Observations
on the Market of Stocks

Observations on the Market of Stocks

John R. Hansen

iUniverse, Inc.
New York Lincoln Shanghai

Observations on the Market of Stocks

iUniverse, Inc.

For information address:
iUniverse, Inc.
2021 Pine Lake Road, Suite 100
Lincoln, NE 68512
www.iuniverse.com

ISBN: 0-595-30319-6 (Pbk)
ISBN: 0-595-66152-1 (Cloth)

Printed in the United States of America

Contents

Preface

Merely reading this Book will not increase your wealth; nor will the application of the information it contains guarantee you riches from the market of stocks. However, if you use these observations to become an investor or trader dedicated to the thoughtful study of this very challenging subject, you will succeed more often than you will fail. And in the market of stocks that is a respectable achievement.

I want to thank my son Robert G. Hansen, a recent graduate of the Carroll School of Management at Boston College for his input, and also my friend and professional economist, Dan M. Bechter, PhD for assistance and encouragement at a critical juncture in this project. My editors at iUniverse provided course correction and proofreading necessary for the production of this Book. And importantly, I give credit to the many authors quoted as part of the foundation for my observations.

I solicit information or experiences that have proven useful to you, the reader, as an investor or trader. *Observations on the Market of Stocks* is a work in progress. Credit will be given in future editions to each reader who helps to expand the scope and increases the usefulness of this Book. You may contact the author at www *Insightpublications.biz*.

This Book is dedicated to my children; Kristi, John and Robert, and their offspring, in the hope that my mistakes will be their instruction; and to my wife, Karen, who only helped me with this Book but has stood by me in failure and encouraged me in success.

Introduction

Post-1999 Bear Market

The long and powerful bull market of the 1990's made the reality of a bear market a dim memory for experienced investors and a non-existent fantasy to millions of financial neophytes. Both groups eagerly poured billions of dollars into the market of stocks during that decade through mutual funds, individual retirement accounts, contributory qualified retirement plans and as personal investments. They were encouraged in this by enlistees in the army of financial advisors who prodded and promoted the bull during those heady years.

Reaction to the Bear

After such an extended bull run, the bear market that began in the spring of 2000 was accompanied by surprise and dismay. As portfolio values dwindled, and 401K funded retirement dreams were shattered, the typical response became, "This can't be happening to me." The effect of the bear market on the psyche of investors who continued to hold common stocks as the cornerstone of their assets was the financial version of Chinese water torture. You may have experienced this pain. During 2003, however, the market of stocks staged a dramatic turnaround. The major stock indexes rose between 15% and 50% since the beginning of that year and hundreds of stocks on the Nasdaq have seen their prices double, triple and more from their March lows.

Participating in the market of stocks

Whether you are an investor, a trader, or both, these observations are written to help you participate successfully in both a bear and a bull market.

Observation

The label, "bull" or "bear" applied to the market of stocks at any point in time should be an important guide to your investing or trading strategy. But the label alone must not dictate your strategy because it will never define the direction in price for all stocks. During the late great bear market, some sectors such as precious metals, and some individual stocks, Sovereign Bank Corp for one, advanced nicely. Likewise, during the bull market that began in 2003 legendary winners of the past, drug companies Johnson and Johnson and Merck, for example, and several of the "Baby Bells" split off from AT&T, such as SBC and Verizon, lost ground.

Definition of investor and trader

For purposes of this Book, an investor is a person who initiates transactions in the market of stocks to realize *long-term capital gains* for tax purposes. This means that the stocks you buy as investments must be held for at least twelve months. An investor will rely primarily on the economic performance of a Company, expressed as "fundamentals," to move the price of its stock upward.

On the other hand, a trader initiates transactions in the market of stocks to realize *short-term capital gains*, i.e., stocks will be bought and sold more frequently than after a one year holding period. A trader will rely primarily on the positive or negative enthusiasm of other buyers and sellers of a Company's stock to move its price upward or downward. The trader will find opportunities in stocks that are moving up simply because they are moving up, or down simply because they are moving down. Such moves are driven by "momentum."

To summarize, if you invest in a stock you will focus on economic factors that will cause it to advance in price, and you will hold those stocks for at least a year. Regarding the stocks you intend to trade, you will focus on the sentiment expressed by both investors and other traders toward those stocks and their price movements.

As a trader you will also borrow shares of stock and sell them with the expectation of re-purchasing those shares at a lower price so they can be returned to the lender. This "short sale" transaction is discussed in Chapter 2.

Opportunity for the investor

Investors should remember the Stoic's philosophy, "This too, shall pass" in dealing with a bear market decline in portfolio values; and when the market turns, investors should resist the temptation to ignore fundamentals and chase stocks that levitate in defiance of their financial field of gravity.

Great fortunes have been made by the accumulation of stocks with sound fundamentals during both bull and bear markets and the retention of these stocks for a lifetime. The purchase of such stocks with a fixed amount of money each month or each quarter, the "dollar cost averaging" method of investing, has served many investors very well.

Observation

A bear market presents a prime opportunity for an investor to acquire desirable stocks at depressed prices. Investors who set aside cash for investment in undervalued stocks and invested that money since March 2003 have enjoyed good fortune. And if you diversified your financial investments into good quality bonds during the bear market you have also enjoyed significant benefits. The Federal Reserve's repeated reductions in interest rates prior to the late summer of 2003 created an historic bull market in mid-term and long-term bonds because the price of these investments moves inversely to interest rates. That is to say, when interest rates decline, the price of bonds advance.

Opportunity for the trader

Astute traders welcome a bear market as an opportunity to sell short. Overnight riches rewarded short sellers in October 1987 when the Dow Jones Industrial Average dropped 22.6% in one day. While such a crash event did not occur in the post-1999 bear market, a slow decline of even greater magnitude did occur in all of the major stock market indexes.

Observation

A short sell, step back and relax strategy during the late great bear market was very profitable. A trader looking for more action during a bear market can also ride the nearly vertical but short-duration up moves that truncate the prevailing price downtrends.

Professional traders' effect on the market

Professional traders, generally the first group to put their financial finger in the wind to discover a change in market direction, provided much of the buying power behind the bull market that began in 2003. Investors, responding to this up trend in prices, took shares off the table to rebuild portfolios. The result in the early stages of a bull market is a reduced supply of available stock sought after by an increased number of buyers. This is a recipe for serious price advances.

Purpose and theme of this Book

In addition to the purpose of helping you understand the market of stocks so that you can select stocks which will deliver superior returns, an underlying theme of this Book is to emphasize the importance of protecting your capital by keeping it under control (UC) rather than having it spin out of control (OC). You will see these abbreviations throughout this Book to remind you of this theme. Whether you act as an investor or as a trader, UC and OC are always relevant concepts. These observations are meant to help you keep your capital UC, thereby improving your chances for success in the market of stocks[*].

---

[*] The phrase "market of stocks" was coined by John McGee, co-author with Robert D. Edwards of their seminal work, *Technical Analysis of Stock Trends*, a book which is now in its Eighth Edition, (2001) published by the American Management Association, W.H.C. Bassetti, editor. *Technical Analysis of Stock Trends* is cited here as "*TAST*."

A friend suggested that the title of this book should be, "*Observations on the Market for Stocks*." I disagree. The phrase "Market *of* stocks" implies a place where plenteous equity offerings are on the table with promising potential for profit. A "Market *for* Stocks", on the other hand is a dry and empty phrase; a facility for commerce is present but without the goods, the hopes and the dreams.

I. Investment Advisors

There is an old saw, "A lawyer who takes his own case has a fool for a client." This advice could be given to any investor or trader who keeps solely his or her own counsel.

A. Obtaining investment advice

It is difficult to make money buying and selling shares of common stock. Therefore, seeking advice on how to best to invest or trade is only prudent (UC). But if you enter the investment advice marketplace, beware! Legions of for-hire money managers are in fall-back careers from the ranks of the unemployed or the unemployable. And investment newsletters that promise to make their subscribers an instant fortune are a large component of the financial junk mail that, along with credit card solicitations, should wind up in your circular file (UC).

1. *Value of free advice.* Un-requested free advice you receive by snail or e-mail that recommends one or more specific investment opportunities is generally worth its price. This is especially true when the fine print reveals that the sender has received money and options, or perhaps even

7

shares of stock, as compensation to prepare and mail the tout sheet. And stock recommendations that come via telemarketers even more probably will prove to be losers (OC).

Observation

Once in a great while, an investment newsletter editor will mail marginally reliable free information as a hook to get new subscribers. If you are attracted to one of these recommendations, put the stock on your watch list and wait for a price decline. Then research the news that prompted the mailing. If the news has real substance, you may then consider buying the stock.

2. *Selecting an investment publication*. Before relying on any investment publication for guidance on the purchase or sale of specific stocks, you should document the publication's track record. A good resource for this purpose is the *Hulbert Financial Digest*. This newsletter, published by Mark Hulbert, compiles results of past recommendations of many investment advisories available to the public by subscription.

Observation

The American Association of Individual Investors, 625 North Michigan Avenue, Chicago, IL 60611-3110, provides many useful and generally reliable investment publications and seminars for the small investor. The AAII is a Code Section 501(c)(3) non-profit public education organization with no mouths to feed.

3. *Selecting an investment advisor.* Interview a prospective personal money manager rigorously before relying on proffered investment advice or entrusting that person with your money.

    (a) *Credentials.* Make certain your interviewee is registered with the Securities and Exchange Commission (SEC) under the 1940 Investment Advisor Act as investment advisor and has passed either the Level 7 or Level 66 exam given by the National Association of Securities Dealers. This credential does not ensure skill but it shows a person's commitment to study the market of stocks. The advisor you select also should have demonstrated additional technical skills by becoming a Certified Financial Planner (CFP) or Chartered Financial Advisor (CFA) (UC).

    (b) *Track record.* Before you engage an investment advisor, require the person to prove success through disclosure of their portfolio results, or the results for current clients on a no-name basis, over a several year period. "What is your track record?" is a very appropriate inquiry. You should reject out of hand any potential advisor who is not able to document successful performance to your satisfaction.

4. *Basis for advice.* Your investment advisor must state cogently and persuasively the rationale for a recommendation that you purchase or sell a specific stock. If the reasons for action are unclear or contradictory, you should question the recommendation. A failure to ask questions can be harmful to your financial health (UC).

Observation

An investment recommendation that does not incorporate financial statement information is frequently unreliable advice (OC). Advice from the "Isn't she a dandy stock," school does not impress experienced investors. They will say, "Show me the numbers."

5. *Terminating the relationship.* If your investment advisor or newsletter nearly always advises a "buy" or "hold" and rarely advises a sell, look for a different advisor or newsletter.

B. Stockbrokers

A stockbroker (or a mutual fund salesman) is a person whose standard of living depends upon the commissions paid by clients.

Observation

The investor or trader's ability to buy and sell stocks over the Internet has exposed the inefficiencies inherent in using a personal stockbroker. To justify their existence, brokerage firms are now re-casting stockbrokers as "financial consultants" and training them to communicate to clients using terms like "portfolio balancing" and other trendy concepts. If you ask one of these newly minted investment experts for one *original* purchase recommendation, generally the answer will be that stock picking is left to the professional money managers employed by or affiliated with the employer. The old time stockbroker who thought for himself, took portfolio risks right along side his clients, and offered profitable advice based on acumen and judgment, is rapidly disappearing from the scene.

1. *Ignoring advice.* A stockbroker who agrees with every transaction you propose and encourages immediate action is operating on the premise that a transaction deferred is a commission lost (OC). Give such a stockbroker's self-serving advice little weight in your investment decisions. On the other hand, a stockbroker who questions your decisions that would otherwise result in a commission may be a reliable advisor.

2. ***Interacting.*** Even if your stockbroker is objective and demonstrates skill and empathy, as a general rule it is best to not combine social and customer-broker relationships. Avoid creating a personal relationship that may implicitly require you to please the other person.

3. ***Executing orders.*** Transactions executed over the Internet on a discount brokerage firm's website insulate the investor or trader from bogus advice and self-serving suggestions. But the greatly reduced commissions on Internet trades (in the order of 90% less than "full service" commissions"), and the instant gratification from immediate execution, may lead you to engage in excessive and impulsive stock dealings (OC). Remember, second thoughts cannot reverse a buy or sell order initiated by a mouse click. Review your orders and the expected proceeds carefully before pulling the trigger. This pause for reflection is a distinct advantage to trading or investing on the Internet vs. telephone instructions to a stockbroker whose time means money.

4. ***Promotions.*** There was a time when stockbrokers promoted stocks recommended by their employers to customers regardless of investment merits or suitability for the customer. But in 2003, on this score the proverbial excrement hit the air

motility device. As reported by AP in the *Trenton Times* on May 8, 2003,

> The regulators have exposed Wall Street's culture in an investigation that found analysts misled investors with stock picks designed to win the firm's investment-banking business issuing the stock.

As a result of both the imposition of fines and adverse publicity, the broker's practice of pushing stock favored by their employer for its business reasons has been curtailed. But will this practice end? The newspaper article quoted above opened with the following paragraph:

> Skeptical senators questioned regulators yesterday about whether a $1.4 billion settlement with 10 big investment banks would lead to real change on Wall Street or benefit ordinary investors and if top brokerage executives would be held accountable.

While the game of pushing employer-touted stock into retail customers' portfolios has been slowed by the "admit no wrongdoing but pay 1.4 billion dollar settlement," it is unlikely that all of the improper promotion will be put permanently on the sidelines.

C. Pooled portfolio trading

Some stockbrokers promote the services of money managers who pool the capital of a number of customers with "similar" investment goals and risk tolerance. The customer is asked to give the manager discretionary trading authority over their account and to pay a fee for the manager's supposed money management expertise. What the customer does not realize is that the manager's "discretion" will be exercised by the use of a computerized trading program using built-in price and volume triggers to automatically initiate transactions. When buy or sell transactions are simultaneously executed in several customers' accounts, it is called, "pool trading."

Why would a stockbroker recommend pool trading for a customer's account? If a number of accounts are pool traded by a discretionary money manager for a fee paid by the customers, the brokerage firm, and its stockbrokers, share indirectly in that fee. Managers who trade frequently pay large total commissions. Customers with investment portfolios trade infrequently and pay small total commissions.

1. *Churning.* The pooled portfolio is churned unmercifully. Short-term odd lot purchases and sales appear by the hundreds on the customer's annual brokerage statements (OC). To add insult to injury, every single computer-driven trade from a pool trading account must be listed on

Schedule D of the customer's Form 1040 as a capital gain or loss. The intention of customers who wanted to be investors rather than traders is thwarted.

2. *Losing capital.* Invariably, frequent rotation of stocks in a pooled portfolio creates net short-term capital losses. The market of stocks is generally one half or even a whole step ahead of the manager's computer programmers who are striving like Hermes to deliver gains to their supplicants. Since the managers rarely if ever sell short, their trading activities are doomed to failure from the outset (OC). For short-term trading to be successful, the trader must use both long buys and short sales.

Observation

Tax benefits will not bail out a pooled portfolio's losses. The deductible amount of the net capital losses is limited to $3,000 per year. Unused losses are carried-over to be added to next year's losses, and the loss carryover from that year will further bloat the loss carryover to the following year, etc., etc.

3. *Losing dividends.* No attention is given to holding dividend-paying stocks in a pooled portfolio until the ex-dividend date each quarter. If the computer program dictates, "sell" the stock is sold and the dividend goes to the next owner.

Regular cash flow from dividends is not achieved in pool trading.

Summary Observation

Seeking investment advice is a bit like praying. You will get an answer but it may not bring the results you desired.

II. Your Competition

Each stock trades in an individual market populated by a coterie of stock watchers, located in both the US and foreign countries, with millions if not billions of dollars available to them for use in stock market operations. These self-appointed or employer-appointed experts continually buy and sell shares or in other ways influence the market of stocks every hour of every day.

Throughout this Book, each self-appointed or employer-appointed expert who derives a livelihood or compensation from participating directly or indirectly in transactions in the market of stocks is referred to as an, "AE". This is the acronym for "appointed expert."

As a trader, you must recognize that you are competing in every transaction with AEs who are largely responsible for the volatility in the price of every stock.

As an investor, you must recognize that the direction in the price of any stock is largely a result of AE decisions.

A. Respect the competition

As shown in the following excerpts, the average individual investor or trader must take AE competition in the market of stocks *very* seriously.

What individual investors should always recognize is that investing is a professional endeavor, just like the professional golf tour. The market, like the New York City Marathon, is one of the few places where professionals (AEs) and non-professionals interact. It is not a casually approached endeavor...recognize that you are interacting with and competing against people who are on top of the markets all day long. In effect, you are teeing it up with scratch golfers and you've got a 10 (or 20!) handicap. If you really want to participate at the same level and to the same degree, recognize that it takes more than scanning. It takes discipline, it takes time, and it takes effort. Your competition is putting in 40, 50 or 60 hours per week. (Laszlo Birinyi, global trading strategist for Deutsche Bank Securities, "Our Cold Reality" *Personal Finance*, February 2003, 24.)

Investors will get smarter and smarter, starting with those who learn what this book has to say. The professionals (AEs) will stay one step ahead of them, because they are preternaturally cunning and because they spend all their time figuring out how to keep ahead of the public. Edwards and McGee *TAST*, 4.

When you enter the stock market, you are going into a competitive field in which your evaluations and opinions will be matched against some of the sharpest and toughest minds in the business. You are in a highly specialized industry in which there are many different sectors, all of which are under intense study by men whose economic survival depends upon their best judgment. Quote from John Magee cited in Edwards and McGee *TAST*, 2.

B. Identity of the AEs

The group of AEs for any particular stock include the specialist who has been given a privileged trading position in the stock by a regulated securities exchange and the specialists' confidants; analysts working for investment banking and brokerage firms; the management and directors of corporations issuing the stock; and professional individual traders. Also not to be omitted from the AEs are the fund managers and analysts employed by the thousands of publicly traded mutual funds, and the managers and analysts of an unknown, but large number of private partner hedge funds.

Observation

The potential impact of AEs affiliated with hedge funds is huge. These unregulated investment partnerships are now estimated to control over 600 billion dollars. With the shrinkage of the IPO (Initial Public Offering) market, many investors, who formerly placed stock bets through venture capitalists, have turned to the managers of the proliferating hedge funds to wager for them in the market of stocks. These investors are vicarious AEs (OC).

C. Characteristics of the AEs

A successful AE focuses on making money. This vocation is conducted for more than job or retirement security; many AEs define their self-worth by their relative success or failure in the market of stocks. As a result, making money is essential to the psychological health of a number of AEs, and this forces them to be as tough as nails in their work.

Observation

An AE is out to take every advantage of the person on the other side of the transactions the AE initiates. The result is that AE psychic vibrations permeate the trading atmosphere surrounding each stock. Those vibrations can influence the investing public to act emotionally, even irrationally at times, and totally against their best interests (OC). The individual investor is vulnerable to this trap.

D. Characteristics of the investing public

How can the public be so easily gulled by the AEs? A large segment of the public is timorous and fickle. These folks buy a stock and don't know why. They sell a stock and then they cry; fold when they should hold and act impulsively on projections carefully crafted by AE securities analysts. And the public is most responsive to tips based on "inside" information purveyed by customer representatives working for brokerage firms, family members, friends, casual acquaintances, and even total strangers.

Observation

The weak mindedness of the investing public plays right into the hands of the mentally tough and disciplined AEs and the commission men who feed on the public investors' transactions the AEs instigate (OC).

E. How to compete

How can you compete in the market of stocks? You must insulate yourself from the environment that the AEs weave like a visible information web and invisible force field to entrap your money. In the face of this manipulation and the blandishments of self-serving securities, mutual fund and variable life insurance salespersons, frequently the most beneficial advice is, "Don't just stand there! Do nothing" (UC).

1.　***Best decision***. Most of the time, when presented with an investment or trading "opportunity", even one of your own devising, the best decision you can make is no decision. A constructive mindset to adopt when pressure mounts to agree with either: your own quickly formed opinion, a promoter's suggestion, or a crowd at the buying or selling window is, "I don't have to do a damn thing" (UC).

Example

The stock in a Company with a recognized name, at a going out of business price, frequently presents opportunities. I observed the demise of Aquila, the renamed venerable Kansas City electrical utility, Utilicorp. As a result of a disastrous foray into the energy trading game, Aquila's stockholder equity was nearly wiped out and problems with regulators and creditors caused both a Board of Directors migraine and a management shuffle. In the space of a year, the stock dropped from the high thirties to just over a $1.00.

I caught Aquila on the rebound at 1.95 per share, watched it go to 3.05 and then rode it back down. At what turned out to be the nadir of the decline six months later, I arose one morning feeling disgusted with this investment for no particular reason. Without checking for positive or negative news or looking at a stock chart, I gave in to this emotion and made a snap decision to dump the stock.

I felt a certain satisfaction, even a sense of control, when I told my broker to sell. "At market?" he asked. "Yes," I answered deliberately. The day after liquidating my position at 2.22 I watched the shares start up. Two weeks later the stock hit 3.60. The AEs no doubt felt the energy flow from me to them as a result of my impetuous decision to sell out at the bottom. And this was after setting down my observations on the folly of precipitous action! Do you see how easy it is to get mousetrapped in the market of stocks?

2. *Second best decision.* An investor or trader who is not an AE must execute transactions relatively infrequently and use only a part of their capital in each transaction.

Observation

"Traders die broke" is a well-known adage. My version of this rule is, "If you go for broke, you will be broke" (UC).

3. *Third best decision.* Take the opposite course of action from that promoted by the financial information system (UC).

F. AE short sales

You should be aware that AE traders and hedge fund mangers operating on their analysts' recommendations are aggressive short sellers. In other words, they borrow stock and sell it with the expectation that a decline in price will occur. When a short seller repurchases the shares at the lower price and returns them to their original owner, the short seller realizes a short-term capital gain.

Observation

Borrowing stock before selling it short has been a rule frequently observed in the breach by some AEs. "Naked shorts" have become SOP for many hedge funds in their market operations. In effect, selling shares without borrowing can create an unlimited supply of stock for sale. The SEC, under its new Chairman, Wm. Donaldson, a streetwise regulator whose practical experience has been glaringly absent in prior SEC Chairmen, finally issued a proposed rule in October 2003 that would prohibit naked shorts.

1. *AE advantages.* Many AEs have almost unlimited ability to borrow stock from street accounts like Cede & Co. Public investors are required to allow NYSE traded stock held in their accounts at brokerage firms to be transferred to Cede & Co. for this purpose. Nasdaq shares are held at a similar

street account bearing the acronym, DET. The AEs borrow the stock from the public, and then may sell the borrowed stock back to unsuspecting investors who are adding to their positions.

2. ***Specialist participation.*** Specialists, who technically are under an obligation to incur losses if necessary to keep an "orderly market" in assigned stocks, view short selling as being consistent with that privileged position. The specialist, as well as the other AE short sellers, frequently crushes a rally with the best of intentions...to make a profit. To augment their profits when the shorts are taking control AEs also can become put option buyers or call option sellers (OC). The trading of stock options is discussed in detail in Chapter X.

After the short sale, the AE who is either a specialist on a regulated exchange, or is a "market maker" on Nasdaq, invests the proceeds from the sale of the borrowed shares in US Treasury bills for a risk free investment. If the stock sold short pays no dividends, the short sale of that stock has zero carrying cost and gives the AE a risk free investment portfolio paying US government interest.

Observation

There is an anomaly under present tax law related to dividends paid on stock that has been sold short. The short seller may claim an unlimited miscellaneous itemized deduction for the payment of dividends to lenders of the stock. The deduction offsets income taxed to the short seller at ordinary rates up to 35%. This argues against permitting the lender of stock that is borrowed and sold short from being taxed at only a 15% rate on those dividends.

3. *Limits on short sellers.* The SEC rule is that the most recent sale of stock prior to the short sale must have shown an up tic in the price. However, as explained by Richard Ney in his classic work, *The Wall Street Gang*, (Preager Publishers, Inc., 1974), specialists are able to legally circumvent the corollary, "No short sale after a down tic" rule. Market makers in the Nasdaq stocks, who are linked together in a proprietary electronic network styled as the "Nasdaq Stock Market," may also be able to sidestep this rule.

   Other AEs who are in a position to use short sales to drive down the price of a stock, recognize that the SEC's surveillance resources are woefully inadequate to monitor stock trades sufficiently to enforce the up tic rule. In any case, if a broker is caught in a violation, there is a hand slap and it is back to business (OC).

Observation

In theory, a stock market is a physical location where buyers and sellers of shares of stock meet to do business directly with each other or through their agents. In the Nasdaq network, the owners of the computer terminals that make up the market totally control the contact between buyers and sellers, and these players regularly insert themselves into the transaction as a "principal" to make more than a mere commission on the trade (OC). To keep everything above board of course, the broker will be duly noted on the trade confirmation slip acting as "principal" for the customer on the order. This documentation results in after-the-fact approval by a customer who is unlikely to complain about the practice.

But the "acting as principal" scheme by no means is limited to dealings on the Nasdaq. Even transactions in stocks listed on the New York Stock Exchange can appear on the trade confirmation slip as a buy *from the broker* as principal.

4. *First effect of short selling.* Short sales artificially increase the supply of stock during every rally in a bear market and are the chief method used to demoralize the investors who get sucked into the rally at its apex. The result is that a bear market feeds upon itself when discouraged investors follow

the short sellers by dumping stock after the rally fizzles out (OC).

5. *Follow-on effects of short selling.* When a rally is shut down by short selling, the desperation of investors to get out of stock with a declining price may grow intense enough to ultimately result in what is known as a "selling climax." This climax is marked by much greater than normal volume in the stock and an apparent free fall in its price, as the specialist who is charged with the responsibility to keep an orderly market sidesteps his obligation to buy (OC). After the free fall is over, or perhaps as the cause of its termination, short sellers move en masse to purchase the stock in order to lock up their profits. The result is a wild gyration upward in the price of the recently plummeting stock. The financial press frequently explains this phenomenon by saying, "Investors have returned to the market."

6. *Bear raids by short selling.* Even if investors are generally not selling a stock aggressively, short sellers can push its price down. A small volume up tic can be followed by a short sale at a lower price on many more shares. Repeated short sales in this manner on the way down, explain why a stock may fall out of bed disproportionately to the bad news about the company that has disenchanted investors.

7. ***Short sales "against the box."*** AEs are frequently long the same stocks that they are shorting. This permits them to short out a rally in the price of the stock they own, i.e., go short against the box, on day 1 and then on day 2 offer to sell shares of that stock from their long portfolios on the open of the day at a price significantly lower than the close on day 1. This gapping down tactic is designed to send a message to the public, "The immediate rally is over and it would be prudent to sell now in order to preserve your gains." Of course if the public takes the bait and sells, the price of the stock is driven down and this sets up potential profit for the AE short sellers (OC).

G. Magnitude of short selling

No investor should under-estimate the volume of short selling or its impact on the market of stocks. Lauren Rudd, a well-known writer on investments stated on 8/21/02 in the *Trenton Times*, "Wall Street succumbed to profit taking and short selling yesterday (8/20/02). Most of the selling was attributable to short sellers betting the market will retreat a bit over the next couple of days." On the day in question, 8/20/02, the DJIA dropped 118.72 points or 1.32% and the Nasdaq dropped 17.95 or 1.29%. 1,320,620,000 shares were traded on the NYSE.

H. Information on short sales

Under current SEC rules, when a sell order is entered the seller must indicate on the order whether or not it is a short sale. This enables the broker to wait for the required up tic transaction before filling the order. But nothing is done with these data! It would be a simple matter to collate and short sale information on a daily basis. The SEC would do investors a great favor by issuing a rule requiring regulated stock exchanges to publish the volume of shares sold short each day on each traded stock.

1. *Unavailability of short selling information.* Daily information on short sales in the stocks assigned to a specialist is available to that AE and those persons with whom he shares it. But the investing public has no access to daily short sales data. The playing field with respect to this vital information is not level. The response to the obvious inequity by the SEC, the NYSE and other regulated exchanges is to enshroud the knowledge disparity between the AEs and the public with the thunders of silence. Twice a month, the brokerage industry gratuitously submits data on total outstanding shares sold short at the close of the market on a date two week previous (OC). Amazingly, this is the sum total of the information given to the investing public on short selling, the single most influential factor on the direction and price of most stocks.

Observation

In addition to short sales, another bit of important information unavailable to the public is the current fluctuation in shareholder head-count for publicly traded companies. These data are known month by month to AEs in management in advance of the publication of the Company's annual report. This information can be a key determinant for propitious action. Whether the number of common shareholders is expanding or contracting is an indication of the future direction of the Company's stock price.

2. *Value of current short selling information.* An increase in short sales in a stock should be taken as a warning to avoid that stock, because AEs are on the prowl and will not allow the price of the stock to advance. Contrariwise, when the short interest is shrinking, the stock has probably seen its immediate trading bottom and will experience an upswing fueled by short covering and an absence of the artificial supply of stock that short sellers bring to the table (UC).

I. AE trading tactics

AEs who trade for their own account or have discretionary authority to trade in a client's account understand that an annualized 5% gain compounded on a daily basis for 142 days will result in a 1,000% growth in capital. Therefore, long gains are rarely allowed to ripen in AE traders' portfolios as they purchase and sell stock in order to quickly compound small gains. Shorts are sometimes a different story. With short proceeds safely tucked away in Treasury bills if an AE views a stock as headed downward, a short position may be kept open and added to over several months, until the investors in the stock begin bailing out in large numbers.

1. *Chasing stock.* The AE trader will not generally chase a stock except to close a short position. Sometimes, AEs will put in a buy order on the open that is above the prior day's closing price to acquire a small number of shares of a stock they already own. This gap up on the open is an attempt to initiate investor interest in the stock and cause a further up move. If this move occurs it may enable the AEs to subsequently unload a larger number of shares purchased previously at a lower price.

2. *Comparison-shopping.* The AE trader always compares the upside potential among the stocks in the same sector over which he or she is an expert, and will move capital from one issue to another based on this comparison. This game of money musical chairs enables the stocks in a "hot" sector to move smartly up one after another until all with positive news are trading at a new plateau.

Summary Observation

Lewis Carroll advised readers of Alice in Wonderland to beware the jabberwocky, a mysterious nocturnal creature that lived life at the expense of its fellow inhabitants of Wonderland. A similar word of caution can be applied to your dealings with many of the AEs who have appointed themselves experts over every publicly traded stock. On the other hand, some AEs are like the White Rabbit who can lead you to excitement, challenges and perhaps, financial redemption.

III. Trading

If you trade stocks your goal should be to grow your capital in successive successful transactions. Making money on one trade only to lose it on the next is the mark of a trading failure. A gain transaction offset by a loss accompanied by four commissions will at best freeze your capital and reward only your broker.

A. Obstacles to successful trading

It is extremely difficult for a shareholder who is not an AE to profit from frequent in and out stock transactions. Five percentages are obstacles to economic gain from such trading in stocks (OC).

1. *Commission percentage.* The percentage of the trader's money that disappears in commissions on each side of the dual transaction i.e., a sale followed by a buy, or a buy followed by a sale.

2. *Profit percentage.* The profit percentage on profitable quick trades which is usually less than,

3. *The loss percentage* on losing quick trades combined with the effect of,

4. *The percentage of winning trades.* Even if your percentage of winning trades exceeds the percentage of losing trades, you will generally wind

up with an overall loss due to the percentages in 1, 2 and 3.

5. *Income tax percentage.* Successful trading generates short-term capital gains taxed as ordinary income. Federal income tax is imposed on ordinary income at rates up to 35%. This rate is more than double the 15% rate applicable to long-term gains.

Observation

Limiting the percentage of loss on a trade is more difficult than you might expect. You can set a stop i.e., a pre-selected price point at which the broker is theoretically required to sell your stock to limit the loss. In practice, however, stops may not work. The specialist, despite a commitment to maintain an "orderly" market, often permits a stock to gap down on the open of the market or during the day, sometimes on surprisingly nominal volume. The result is that the price of your stock simply passes through and never comes to rest on the selected stop. The next sale may occur at a much lower price than the stop and that will be the price paid for your stock.

B. Principles for trading

You gotta know when to hold them, know when to fold them, know when to walk away, know when to run...Don Schlitz, *The Gambler* copyright 1978, Writers Night Music.

Trading stocks is a bit like being at a poker table, only there are many more players, and the number of possible games is much greater. Observing the following trading principles will maximize your chances for success.

1. ***Be taciturn.*** The purpose of trading is not to establish bragging rights. To maintain an effective trading rhythm the trader must be taciturn and close-mouthed about his or her transactions.

2. ***Be dispassionate.*** A trader must not amble and shamble through the trading process with emotions on display. Leave your emotions at the door when you sit down to trade (UC). Greed, fear, and the dejection-to-elation roller coaster ride between these emotions, have no place in the mentality of a trader. A successful trader must take intelligent risks by thinking with acuity and conviction but without passion. The only states of mind you should experience with respect to any trade are satisfaction or dissatisfaction. Tell your self, "Well done," or "Not well done," and review the reasons for the result. Whether you make money or lose money on a trade, you always win if you come away from the trade with enhanced knowledge of the trading process. Attain wisdom and wealth will follow—if you have not exhausted your trading capital first.

Observation

Unlike a successful trade, stocks purchased as an investment and subsequently sold for a gain, rightly should bring joy to the investor that exceeds mere satisfaction. The enhancement of your capital through proper investment decisions can liberate your life from the control of employers or customers who dole out economic benefits strictly quid pro quo.

3. ***Be cautious.*** You should commit only a portion of your available capital to trading, and that portion should be allocated to at least three trading positions at any one time. Cash can be one of those positions.

4. ***Be conservative.*** If you have a winning trade, take some of your capital off of the trading table (UC).

Observation

A winning trade does *not* make you a genius. Do not let success go to your head so that you double up on successive transactions (OC). Any fool can win money from time to time; it takes a smart person to retain the winnings.

5. **Become an investor.** Invest a portion of the gains in the stock you have been trading. This will eliminate regrets from being out of the stock during a subsequent rise in its price. Regrets impede successful

trading. If your success has been truly rewarding, you may even wish to diversify into bonds, precious metals or real estate with part of your trading gains.

Observation

If you pick a winner and you want to lock up gains, liquidation of your entire position may not be necessary. Unless you have reason to believe that the move for a stock is over and the major trend has reversed, sell just enough shares to produce the desired amount of gain. Retain the unsold shares in your investment portfolio.

6. *Be aware.* A trader must focus on stocks where the promise is based on the enthusiasm or disdain i.e., the favorable or unfavorable sentiment, of other buyers toward the stock. A requirement of demonstrated economic performance *should not limit a trader's decisions.* Thus, prime candidates for the trader's portfolio include oversold stocks in a sector that is coming into favor and low-priced stocks that are in play. There are oversold stocks in sectors that are out of favor and they will stay oversold. There are low-priced stocks with no trader or investor recognition. High transaction volume is the key. The trader must go where the action is. Do not dead-end your trading capital in a stock or a market sector that has nominal daily sales volume.

Observation

An investor must focus primarily on fundamentals, as discussed in Chapter V, for any stock considered for purchase. On the other hand, a trader must be ever alert to momentum, i.e., price movements that do not appear to have a cause based on fundamentals. The trader understands that momentum generally leads reported economic performance. Signs of momentum are day-to-day growth in trading volume and changes in the price of the stock before a news trigger is pulled.

However, when a stock continues to run up to triple or more its yearly lows as a momentum play in disregard of the fundamentals, the trader should consider it a candidate for a short sale. Such a stock may have, "Gotten ahead of itself." If the market for a stock is particularly ebullient, the tether between the ultimate price reversal point and its fundamentals can be very long indeed. But when the stock finally reaches the end of its rope, Johnny-come-lately buyers will learn to their dismay that the rope is made of rubber (OC).

7. *Be greedy.* If you cannot reasonably anticipate a 40% to 60% percent gain on a transaction in a short period of time (three months maximum), do not open that transaction. Upon opening a

trading transaction, you must expect to make a 40% to 60% gain. What you visualize you can realize. This rule requires a trader to deal primarily in low-priced stocks, options on higher priced stocks, warrants, or special situations such as an expected takeover.

8. *Be patient.* Bide your time and trade infrequently but with deliberation. If you missed the initial shot out of the barrel taken by a stock, wait for a stall in its price on high volume, and then stake your position *after* the inevitable pullback.

Observation

The number of 40% to 60% appreciation or depreciation opportunities that can reasonably occur within a ninety-day time horizon is generally a small to minute percentage of the universe of thousands of stocks (UC). And the number of these bona fide trading opportunities that come your way will be in direct proportion to the number of low priced stocks, warrants and options on your watch list.

9. *Be deliberate.* Day trading with a goal of a small percentage gain on each transaction increases the number of required decisions on a linear scale, and the potential for losing your capital on a geometric scale (OC). Do not succumb to the lure of the adrenaline rush that rapid fire trading will

induce. It will be far cheaper for you to get that experience from a video game.

Observation

A famous student of the market who made his living as a trader has said:

And right here let me say one thing; After spending many years in Wall Street and after making and losing millions of dollars I want to tell you this: It never was my thinking that made the big money for me. It always was my sitting. Got that? My sitting tight...Men who can both be right and sit tight are uncommon. I found it one of the hardest things to learn. But it is only after a stock operator has firmly grasped this, that he can make big money. *Reminiscences of a Stock Operator*, Edwin Lefevre, John Wiley & Sons, 1994: 68-69 (originally published 1923, George H. Doran and Company based on the life and times of Jesse Lauriston Livermore)

10. *Be observant.* Stocks that are candidates for a short sale will appear to be overbought, i.e., the buyers of the stock are exhausted. However, an overbought condition is not required if the trader is shorting the stock on the anticipation of the release of bad news. Bad news can drop a stock that is already in a bear market and make it swoon to a much lower price level very quickly.

But perceptively anticipating the release of bad news is difficult and requires experience and a practiced judgment (UC).

Example

I have a friend who was a relatively new securities analyst in the telecom equipment sector for a major brokerage house. At the time of the event herein described, this sector has been out of favor for over two years. My friend had a face-to-face interview with the CFO of Lucent when the stock was selling at $1.25 down from a high of $55.00. He came away from the meeting believing that the Company had probably seen the worst. *The following week* Lucent announced massive bad debt losses on installment sales of equipment. The price of the stock dropped in half. As the stock languished below a dollar, rumors flew of a reverse split necessary to avoid NYSE de-listing. At the meeting with my friend immediately before this cascade of bad news, Lucent's CFO, like a good poker player, revealed no hint of the impending crises.

Observation

After the weak sisters were separated from their Lucent stock because they acted in panic on the bad news (OC), a process that took about six weeks, the stock subsequently tripled in value within a short time. The de-listing rumors were forgotten.

11. ***Be analytical.*** How "bad" is the "bad" news? You may read a silver lining between the lines. If this is the worst punch that the opponent can throw, and the fighter is still on his feet, he may still win in the next round! But is it the worst punch?

   Some of the most harmful punches in both the fight ring and the stock market are the low blows. A prime example of this is the class action lawsuit brought for the "benefit of shareholders." These blows have the potential for large damage awards resulting from something as inconsequential as an incomplete press release. The attorneys who file these suits stand to make millions, while the shareholders lose mega millions in absolute or opportunity costs as their stock flounders under a cloud of uncertainty while the suit is pending.

   However, most class action suits ultimately settle, and at the announcement of a resolution of the case, the stock will respond strongly to the upside. Traders who are sufficiently perspicacious to anticipate a settlement (UC), or who have inside information about it, know when to buy.

12. ***Be a loner.*** As a trader, if you wait for a completed "Head and Shoulders," "Triangle," or any of a number of chart patterns to be fully revealed for a

particular stock, it is very probable that you will be waiting in a crowd. When the pattern is complete, the contrarians in the crowd may act together unwittingly to cause the expected post-pattern move in the price of the stock to abort. A successful trader will not wait for the crowd to yell "charge."

13. ***Be a student.*** To be successful, a trader should look for patterns of oscillation in the price of a stock and not for a cookbook, structural chart formation. Traders must ask these questions, (a) "What is the price level at which buying support will stop a decline ("support level") in a one or two month time horizon for this stock, and (b) what is the price level where available supply will overwhelm the buyers ("resistance level) i.e., where will the short sellers start to blitz?" Only after these questions are answered with some sense of certainty can the trader reasonably pick entry and exit points for trades. A trader should always at least tentatively project the support level and the resistance level in his or her mind *before* taking action (UC).

Observation

The pattern of a stock price chart never replicates a sine wave. But neither is the price pattern of individual stocks merely random, as the author of the book, *A Random Walk Down Wall Street*, (Norton & Company, 1999), B.G. Malkiel, would have you believe. Professor Malkiel accurately demonstrates the failings of both financial and fundamental analysis, and has shown that, in general, managed mutual funds do not outperform the market. However, this does not mandate randomness in the price behavior of stocks. There are many structural impediments to the trading and investing operations of mutual funds that do not apply to individuals. These impediments start with the prospectus that defines and circumscribes a fund's investment portfolio, continue with the size of the transactions that can be closed without disrupting the market, and finish with the inherent conservatism of fund managers, whose first priority is to keep their jobs. To extrapolate the failure of the majority of managed mutual funds to beat general market indices as a curse on individual traders, or investors, is unrealistically discouraging.

As a trader, you should visualize the pattern that a struck tuning fork makes when viewed on an oscilloscope in extremely slow motion. When the tuning fork is struck, the amplitude of the wave rises to its maximum. Over time, the amplitude of the wave decreases, and finally as the sound dies down, the wave comes to a point.

A stock rising in price is illustrated by the axis of the oscilloscope image parallel to earth tilting so as to incline left to right while the oscillations remain vertical. A stock falling in price is illustrated by the axis of the oscilloscope image parallel to the earth tilting so as to decline left to right while the oscillations remain vertical. Of course, the oscillations in a stock's price are not as regular in either amplitude or periodicity along a centerline as the oscillations of sound produced by a tuning fork. But this analogy can be helpful in visualizing the probable course of the price of a stock.

Stocks become "struck" from time to time and the subsequent trading pattern may reflect the tuning fork analogy. Successful traders attempt to ride the upside and downside of several oscillations (UC).

Anticipating the news that will "strike" a stock and induce oscillations is an art and not a science. Also, do not overlook the movement in the price of the stock itself as "news" with a potentially large impact on future price patterns. Before entering an order to buy or sell a stock, use this model. Visualize in your mind's eye the past and probable future oscillations in the price of the stock. Are you entering your order to buy or to sell at a propitious time in that pattern (UC)?

14. *Be methodical.* The message of the preceding paragraphs is clear; trading stocks is not a shoot-from-the-hip occupation. Successful trades must be carefully planned. You must watch for a pre-selected price point in your target stock before taking action. Do not force a trade. Let the opportunity come to you. Do not initiate a transaction simply to get out of cash or to get into cash (UC).

15. *Be goal-oriented.* You must know when you are taking a position for trading purposes and when you are taking a position for investment (UC). Selling a stock purchased for investment, i.e., to secure long-term capital gains, in order to pocket a quick short-term gain is usually a major mistake.

Observation

Selling a stock to realize a premature gain is frequently followed by the investor's decision to buy a replacement stock. If this is a loser you have added insult to injury. Income tax is imposed at ordinary rates on the short-term gain. Two additional commissions must be paid and the loss on the replacement stock may be realized in a subsequent tax year when it will have no gain to offset. Compare this decimation of capital scenario with simply staying put with your investment that was rising in value. Remember, the best decision is usually no decision when it comes to selling or not selling a stock in your portfolio that is held for investment.

16. ***Be a bear as well as a bull.*** Be solely an investor if you are not willing and psychologically prepared to trade both the long side and the short side of the market (UC). You will not be a successful trader if you only have a "bullish mentality" and lose interest in the game when stocks you own decline in value on the theory that an unwatched pot will boil more quickly (OC).

17. ***Be suspicious.*** The advice, "Buy on rumor, sell on fact" is a tip-off to the leverage of news on the price of any stock. But rumors are not news. Rumors may be planted falsehoods, hopes, fears or fantasy tales that grow with the telling (OC). A trader must not rely on rumors. A trader must consider *probabilities* and act accordingly (UC).

Example

Moody's announces that it is considering a reduction in the bond rating of Duke Energy (DUK). The downtrend in DUK stock turns vertical on the news. But what is the probability that *Moody's* will in fact reduce the bond rating of DUK? And even if the probability is high that *Moody's* will take the threatened action, what is the probability that the market had largely discounted this effect prior to such action and the next move for DUK will be up no matter what *Moody's* does?

The successful trader is constantly weighing the probability that the next news item on his target stock will be good (or bad) and he or she goes long (or short) before that news even becomes a rumor.

18. ***Be rational.*** Do not be superstitious about your trading times, places, equipment, etc. (OC). Talismans that will insure or inhibit your success at trading in the market of stocks do not exist.

19. ***Do not be impulsive.*** Be wary of buying in the first hour or so of the trading day. This is the time for the AEs to gap a stock up or down in an effort to suck the uninitiated into a red herring trend that frequently never develops and often is reversed dramatically in subsequent hours (OC). Wait until an initial move in the stock reverses or stabilizes before entering the fray (UC). *Also, never close one position and immediately thereafter with the proceeds (that cannot even be paid to you for five business days) open a new position (UC).*

C. Frequency of short sales

A trader makes money on a stock sold short when the position is closed, i.e., the short seller must return the stock to the lender before any profit is realized. By the very nature of this rule, and the fact that all gains on short sales are automatically ordinary income for tax purposes, short sale transactions may be initiated frequently by AEs who are professional traders for small profits. A trader who is not an AE will be driven to distraction following this practice. If you want to trade, you should set a 40% to 60% profit goal on both short and long transactions. This goal will not be met easily on shorts. Unless a bear market is raging, for most stocks the near-term downward price swing will not be this severe. Therefore, short sales will be a minority of your transactions (UC).

D. Marketplace liquidity

A trader once called his broker and said, "Sell my shares of XYZ." The broker replied, "To whom?" This is to say that some stocks are much easier to buy than to sell. The number of shares at which a bid can be executed is called the "size" of the market for the stock at that moment in time. If the size for a particular stock is small, and you own a large number of shares, the value of your portfolio must be discounted. This is especially true for stocks that trade in the OTCBB (over the counter bulletin board) market among only a few market makers.

Observation

The trader is always faced with the limitation of "size" in executing orders. This is because the "bid" or "asked" price for any stock is always on the table for only a limited number of shares. For example, Cable and Wireless ADRs are bid at $4.55. But when a sell at market order for 3000 shares is entered to take advantage of this bid price, 300 shares (the "size") is taken at 4.55 and 2,700 shares are sold at $4.54. To test whether the size limitation is real, an "all or nothing" order can be entered.

Low priced stocks with relatively few market makers traded on the Nasdaq or OTCBB can also display a large spread between the bid and asked price. Some brokers discourage their customers from buying so-called "penny" stocks because a wide spread makes it difficult to execute an order at the customer's expected price. The beta of penny stocks can be extremely high with moves of 20% to 30% up or down in a day.

E. Staying in the game

If you want to stay in the trading game you must observe the following principles of capital protection.

1. *Trading because of liquidity.* Never trade simply because you have "buying power" in your account (UC). See subparagraph 19 (Do not be impulsive) above. A trader must have asbestos pockets.

2. *Limit your potential loss.* When you enter a position, whether long or short, establish the maximum acceptable loss at the time of entry. For stocks with a price over $10.00, a twenty five per-

cent loss should automatically close out the deal. Fighting the tape is both an economic and psychological defeat (UC). Low-priced stocks are too volatile for the establishment of an arbitrarily determined stop loss point (UC). These stocks must be considered on a case-by-case basis. When the opening price of the day is well below yesterday's close, this may be evidence of a bear raid designed to shake stock out of the hands of weak sisters into the hands of the AEs who will soon be covering their short sales at the expense of the demoralized sellers. An automatic close out to avoid a predetermined percentage loss could make you the unwitting victim of their strategy.

3. **Stick by your profit goal.** Don't cut and run from a position to gain a small profit in disregard of your planned profit goal exit point (OC). Similarly, don't cut and run from a position if you are experiencing a loss less than your stop. "Protecting your capital" in this manner puts you into the psychic manipulation trap perpetrated by the AEs and will disrupt your trading rhythm (OC).

4. **Profits are capital.** Capital generated from trading profits must be considered just as scarce and worthy of protection as capital from any other source. Do not label profits as "playing with the other person's money" and let down your guard. Put this thought entirely out of your mind. After

you have earned a profit, it is *your* money; it is not on loan from the AEs. However, the profit must be shared with your broker, the IRS and state taxing authorities. If you have the experience of this required sharing on only one April 15th, you will understand that trading stocks is a serious business.

Summary Observation

The trader is in a war. Following the principles of trading outlined in this chapter is your strategy for winning and capital is the ammunition. Losing your capital will lead to defeat. Therefore, capital must be protected. It is the scarcest and most valuable of resources. The trader should relate to capital the way Gollum related to the Ring of Power in JRR Tolkein's masterful epic, *The Lord of the Rings* (New Line Products, Inc., 2001) (UC).

IV. Investing

Investing is a future oriented activity. The investor's commitment of capital to a stock must be for a one-year or longer period. This chapter discusses the mindset of an investor and presents some general investment theories and techniques. Further information on the selection of individual stocks is found in Chapter VII.

A. Mindset of an investor

Successful investors are made, not born; to develop the proper mindset takes discipline and dedication to the task.

1. ***Be Observant.*** To invest profitably, you must pay consistent attention to the stocks you have purchased and to your target stocks. Set up both groups as a portfolio on a website financial page. Review the price, trading volume and chart pattern of these stocks *each and every day* whether you are losing or winning (UC).

2. ***Be Patient.*** It is axiomatic that an investor who is short on patience will be short on profits (OC). Be realistic regarding the time required for a stock you have purchased to attain your objective.

3. **Be rational.** Know your reasons for investing in or disposing of a stock. Test those reasons logically against credible facts. Control your fear. Do not give in to greed (UC). When selling a stock, you should expect the buyer to make money. Trying to squeeze the last bit of profit out of every trade, an impossible goal, is certain to lead to frustration. And frustration causes emotional reactions that will interfere with your decision-making process (OC).

4. **Be purposeful.** You should open each investment position with an annual percentage rate of return objective. Having a defined investment goal will put discipline in your decision making process and focus your attention on investment success (UC). Overcoming the influence of the AEs on your psyche requires that you see yourself as achieving the stated investment goal.

Observation

The third Bush Tax Reduction Act, signed into law on May 28, 2003, reduced the Federal income tax on dividends for both regular and alternative minimum tax purposes to 15%. This is the same rate that is applied to long-term capital gains, i.e., on stocks held over 12 months. The parity between the income tax rate on long-term capital gains and dividends will enable dividend-paying stocks help you to achieve your rate of return of return objective.

5. **Be a student.** Read information about the stocks you own and your target stocks as it becomes available from reliable sources in print and on the Internet (UC).

Example

If you wish to research dividend paying stocks you can refer to *Mergent's Dividend Achievers* published quarterly by Mergent, Inc. This publication presents comprehensive data on the stocks of companies that have increased their dividends each year for ten years or more.

Observation

Future editions of *Dividend Achievers* compared with the May 2003 edition, published just after the tax reduction on dividends was passed, will reveal whether dividend-paying stocks have more appeal in the market of stocks than the shares of companies that eschew dividends. A cursory review of the May edition shows that this has not previously been the case. A majority of the 284 companies compiled by Mergent Inc. as dividend payers *under-performed* the New

York Stock Exchange Composite Index for the 12 months ended in May 2003.

(a) ***Information sources.*** The Internet sites *Sec.gov/edgar.hp.htm* and *Free Edgar.com* will provide you with all corporate filings made with the Securities and Exchange Commission by companies that are publicly traded in the US. Ideally, you should become familiar with the information filed with the SEC by a Company in its most recent quarterly Form 10Q and annual Form 10K before you make a decision to buy the stock of that Company. Canada and its provinces have similar information available at *Sedar.com* pertaining to stocks traded on exchanges located north of the border.

(b) ***Analyzing SEC Filings.*** Reports filed with the SEC incorporate the communicational structure and style required by that bureaucracy. After reading a number of Forms 10Q and 10K you will begin to master the fine art of reading between the lines of these reports. This will enable you to develop valuable insights into the operation of the reporting Company and its probable future prospects (UC).

6. **Be deliberate.** Snap decisions to buy or sell a stock made by even the most seasoned trader or

investor AE are frequently a misadventure. Therefore, you should adopt a rule that under no circumstances will you initiate both a sell and a buy transaction in the same phone call or visit to your Internet broker. "Haste makes waste" is an adage that certainly applies to transactions in the market of stocks (OC). Make your investment decisions only after investigation, examination and deliberation (UC).

B. Risk tolerance

Stocks are only one of several alternative investments for your capital. You must determine your tolerance for risk and need for monetary rewards in deciding what portion of your money to commit to gunplay in the market of stocks. If you see yourself as the hunter rather than the hunted, your tolerance for risk is probably high. If your reward is not monetary gain but winning against competition, your tolerance for risk is even higher, and the market of stocks may then claim the lion's share of your capital. On the other hand, if you need your capital to provide for immediate or anticipated near-term standard of living financial needs, and you do not handle stress outside of the workplace well, then your tolerance for risk is low. In this case, the market of stocks should play a minor role in your financial architecture.

C. Allocation of your capital

You will probably fall somewhere between the high-risk tolerance and the low-risk tolerance poles. And your position between these poles may change over time. This argues for annual decisions on the appropriate allocation of your financial resources to: the market of stocks, secure high rated interest paying securities, precious metals, life insurance and liquid assets. Each year you should review your annual rate of return on investments and the timeline for your expected financial needs. Revise your allocation decisions based on these data when the month for decision rolls around. Rebalance your portfolio by selling assets and reinvesting the proceeds to implement those decisions. This annual review and reprise is a plan that should enable you to live knowing that your capital is not spinning OC but is *marching forward on a directed and rational path* (UC).

Observation

If trading stocks is not your occupation, don't become a Walter Mitty and pretend that it is. Apply only a small portion of your capital to short-term transactions in the market of stocks.

D. Value investing

Value investing is a stock selection method that emphasizes a target Company's balance sheet. Benjamin

Graham (1894–1976), the father of value investing, preached the concept of value investing earnestly in five versions of his book, *The Intelligent Investor,* (Harper Collins, 1997) published between 1946 and 1973. The 1973 fourth revised edition is now available with an introduction and appendix by Graham's most famous student, admirer, and apologist, Warren Buffet. Buffet, the second richest man in the US after Bill Gates and sometimes called the Oracle of Omaha, is the majority owner of the highest priced publicly traded stock, Berkshire Hathaway.

1. ***Importance of tangible net book value.*** If you are a true value investor, you will buy only stocks of companies with a *market capitalization,* i.e., number of shares outstanding times the price per share, which is less than the Company's tangible net book value. Tangible net book value is the stockholder's net equity shown on the right side of the balance sheet minus intangible assets, such as goodwill, which are shown on the left side of the balance sheet.

   To a value investor an even more desirable stock is issued by a Company with a market capitalization that is exceeded by its liquid assets, i.e., the total of cash, inventory, receivables and other cash equivalents shown in asset section on the left hand side of the balance sheet.

2. ***Additional value investing criteria.*** Two further tests for the value investor are whether the

Company has paid dividends continuously for twenty or more years, and whether the Company has had an unbroken string of operating profits for at least ten years.

Observation

Tangible net book value in excess of market capitalization, dividends paid for twenty years and operating profits earned for ten years are stringent tests. After the run-up of the bull market that began in 2003, few if any companies are candidates for the unswerving value investor's portfolio.

3. *Investing for protection of capital.* Graham also espoused a margin of safety concept as part of his theory of value investing. An important test to Graham was whether the net equity of the Company exceeded its debt and also whether the Company's earnings exceeded the interest on its debt. These criteria will be important to an investor whose primary goal is protection of capital rather than growth. Your capital will be protected if you select companies with long term debt that is less than one half of their equity and short-term debt and other current liabilities that is less than the total of their cash, receivables and inventory. Exceptions to the long-term debt to equity ratio rule are companies in a capital-intensive industry such as electric, gas and water utilities (UC).

E. Value investing in practice

Warren Buffet and other very successful money manager/investors who studied at Graham's knee before his death in 1976 continue to be apologists for value investing although in practice their stock investments rarely adhere to all of Graham's criteria.

1.   *Modification of value criteria.* The current US economy is based largely on the sale of services and consumer goods. This requires that balance sheet assets and shareholder equity of many companies be adjusted upward for the value of product or Company recognition, market penetration and expertise.

Example

The financial press occasionally quantifies these items. Thus, for example, the editors of *Business Week* put a value on product and company recognition in the article, "The 100 Top Brands," in the August 4, 2003 issue at page 72. Coca-Cola was the winner of this sweepstakes with a brand value of 70.45 billion dollars. Is it little wonder that value investor Warren Buffet's investment company, Berkshire Hathaway, is the biggest shareholder in Coca-Cola? Number one hundred on the list, with a brand value of 1.61 billion dollars is that fine sipping bourbon, Jack Daniels, produced by the Brown Forman Company.

2. *Value investing myopia.* Benjamin Graham commenced work on Wall Street in 1914 at twenty years young. He never purchased stock in International Business Machines or its predecessor, C-T-R Co., even though by his own admission he had early on recognized the worth of its products. He concluded that there was too much "water" in the form of intangible assets in IBM's balance sheet. It was Graham's view that even after the "water" had been squeezed out of IBM's balance sheet, "A different kind of water has been put back into the valuation by the stock market—by investors and speculators themselves." The fact that IBM was selling at 7 times its published 1957 book value in May 1958, made its stock unacceptable to Graham as an investment. Graham, *The Intelligent Investor*, 317.

Adjusted for splits, IBM's price increased from pennies in 1926, when it changed its name to C-T-R Co., to $15.00 in December 1973, the year Graham published his book for the last time. Twenty-eight years later, in December of 2001, IBM sold for $125.00 per share.

Observation

Graham believed that paying for future growth would expose the average investor to excessive risks. This anti growth stock bias was based on his conviction that future growth in sales and profits was too problematic to be a reliable pricing mechanism for a Company's stock. If the growth did not occur, i.e., the promise was not realized, the market would reject the stock.

Graham's anti growth stock posture certainly was validated during his lifetime before World War II by his experience as a student of both the market of stocks and the economy. But the environment that forms the basis for all economic and investment theories is not static. Time does not stand still in order to accommodate the ideas of any person, no matter how brilliant or insightful they may be.

The following data are instructive:

Year	GNP per Capita Current Dollars	GNP per Capita Inflation Adjusted	Total GNP
1912-16	$408		40.4B
1932	468		58.4B
1939	695		91.0B
1945	1,526		292.2B
1960	2,935	$9,900	1.8T
1975	7,632	14,560	3.1T
2001	35,686	20,163	5.7T

Source: *Historical Statistics of the United States* and *Statistical Abstract of the United States–2002*, US Department of Commerce

The numbers shown in the chart above reflect the dramatic increase in dollar amount of economic transactions between buyers and sellers in the US economy since Graham commenced working on Wall Street in 1914. What the numbers do not reveal is the ever-changing mix of products and services that make up the US Gross National Product. This change has been so revolutionary as to make inflation comparisons of post-960 data with pre-1960 data misleading or inapplicable.

The dollar expansion in the US economy both in terms of raw and inflation adjusted numbers since Graham's death in 1976 makes clear that economic growth has been both exceedingly real and vigorous. Engines of this growth, primarily publicly held companies like IBM that continually reinvent the economy because of the cutting edge nature of their business, have created prosperity for long-term shareholders.

Avoiding "growth stocks" in the boom years since 1974 in fear and trepidation of the future, or a reluctance to study the mechanisms of technological change, may have honored Graham's memory. But that strategy also denied his loyal subjects many opportunities to multiply wealth.

3. ***Graham's continuing influence.*** Graham's teaching has cast a long shadow. In a prospectus dated

August 29, 2003 and issued in conjunction with its effort to raise $150,000,000, the Ivy Multi-Strategy Hedge Fund LLC defined its strategy for investing in stocks as follows:

Equity Investing This strategy involves purchasing securities at prices which, in the Portfolio Manager's opinion are *less than the per share value of the issuers' assets* (emphasis added) or earning power. The *emphasis* of managers pursuing this type of strategy *is on individual stock selection*, (emphasis added) rather than predicting market direction, and the use of fundamental analysis as well as analytical and statistical analysis. *Prospectus, August 29, 2003 as supplemented on September 26, 2003*, Ivy Management Group, a subsidiary of the Bank of New York.

F. Investing for growth

Value investing and investing for growth are not mutually exclusive concepts. An acceptable "growth" stock will necessarily have a substantial base of income producing assets. But in the information age, the rule that such assets must be represented by something "tangible" measured in dollars on the Company's balance sheet is an anachronism. In what account is the Windows program carried on the balance sheet of Microsoft?

In point of fact, the true value of the tangible assets owned by many old line "smoke stack" companies Graham considered as the determinants of an appropriate stock price is now measured only by the tax write-offs they represent. Plant and equipment obsolescence is endemic in an age of unlimited competition from imports. China had no economic significance whatsoever for Graham. Today, WalMart alone imports over 12 billion dollars in goods from that country every quarter and marks these goods up to earn billions in gross profit. Factories in the US that used to manufacture these now imported goods are scrap. On the other side of the coin, companies like Walt Disney and McDonald's that have modest tangible assets have developed value by exporting their products and services to an extent far beyond Graham's imagining.

Observation

Here is a successful investing for growth strategy; identify companies with a product or name franchise that generates growing sales to an expanding customer base. These companies generally make money for their shareholders regardless of the amount of tangible assets on their balance sheets.

Example

In the 1990's bull market stocks with a strong franchise and growing sales included such companies as Johnson & Johnson, General Electric, Wrigley, Colgate, Clorox, Brown Forman, and Home Depot. But the past is not necessarily prologue. The market of stocks is a play with a constantly changing cast of characters. For example, today Starbucks or Panera Bread may hold more promise of future growth than Home Depot.

You and your advisor(s) must think out of the box in selecting stocks that will become the capital growth generators of tomorrow because of their potential for growing sales (UC).

G. Portfolio diversification

The concept of "diversification" is a mantra of current portfolio theory. Indeed, the Prudent Investor Act adopted by most states establishes adequate diversification as a legal standard for fiduciaries wishing to avoid lawsuits of disgruntled beneficiaries. But how much diversification is appropriate in an individual investor's portfolio? And how should "diversification" be defined? There are thousands of equity investment alternatives both as individual stocks and mutual funds. Adding to the diversification challenge is the high noise level emanating from the market of stocks (just watch CNN for a day) and the AE psychic pressure inveigling you to commit funds.

1. **An old hand's advice.** One authority, Gerald Loeb, the erstwhile "Wizard of Wall Street," in his book, *The Battle for Stock Market Profits*, Simon and Schuster, 1971, advised readers to own no more than four stocks at any one time. This is a minimalist investment strategy. Peter Lynch, a modern investment titan, had just the opposite view. He built the Fidelity Magellan fund into one of the most successful mutual funds ever conceived by his purchase and sale of stocks issued by more than a thousand companies.

2. *Concept diversification.* An individual investor should not attempt to create a private mutual fund. But limiting your portfolio to only four stocks is too restrictive. In diversifying your portfolio, diversify your concepts. Thus, you will want to own several stocks with increasing dividends that are reinvested. You will want to own several stocks in sectors of the market that promise growth. And you will want to own stocks that have been beaten down by the vagaries of investment fashion despite the underlying merits of their balance sheets. An arbitrary limit of four stocks is too few to accommodate this strategy. Eight to ten stocks are a more reasonable portfolio headcount.

H. Changes in your portfolio

You should take pride in owning the stocks you have selected for your portfolio, but be ready to shrink that portfolio to protect gains or minimize losses. Review your stock investments annually and weed out shares held for two years that have not attained your rate of return objective. Also, consider the sale of a portion of your position in stocks that have significantly out-performed your rate of return goal on the theory that in the subsequent year the worm will turn. No investor ever went broke taking a profit (UC).

1. ***Protect your capital.*** Protect your capital by selling a stock if you anticipate that the facts initially giving rise to the reasonable prospect of appreciation, i.e., growing dividends, expanding sales, solid financials, etc., *are not expected continue in the future* (UC). Anticipation of this change in the facts, rather than the actual change in the facts, is key. To anticipate requires an awareness of tip-off negatives disclosed by the analysis techniques discussed in Parts V and VI and the extrapolation of these negatives into the future.

2. ***Make the Internet work for you.*** As mentioned previously, you should establish a list of target stocks on an Internet website, such as AOL's personal finance platform, *finance.yahoo*, or with a broker, that permits near real time tracking of the price of your target stocks. In addition to price

information, a good website will provide the latest published news on the Company. At one time, such timely information was available only to the financial services industry and not to the general public. But the Internet has leveled the playing field in this regard (UC). For each target stock you should select a price entry point so that available funds can be efficiently invested.

3. *Portfolio additions.* As an investor, you should hold some capital in a money market account and wait for a downdraft in the price of a target stock. If the downdraft appears to be an irrational response to minimal negative news, the stock should be added to your portfolio (UC).

Observation

Frequently, deep pocket AEs operating in a particular name widely held stock orchestrate a downdraft in its price. Did Cable and Wireless American Depository Receipts (ADRs) with its solid dividend history and $10.00 per ADR book value deserve to get pounded from $4.00 to $1.91 merely on news of a possible breach of contract legal action? Did Lucent at fifty-five *cents*, Nortel Networks at forty-three *cents* or Williams Co. at seventy-eight *cents*, sell for a price that made any sense? Within the year

Nortel reached $4.70, Lucent reached $2.80 and Williams Cos. reached $10.00.

Obviously, in the case of the above big name stocks, the imminent bankruptcy predicted by the penny stock prices was bogus. Too many managers would have lost their jobs in a flame out of these large enterprises. In each case the managers battled mightily to extend their careers, and the result on share prices was predictable.

The resuscitation of these fallen angels is the flip side of IPO after IPO of the 1990's that were nothing but smoke turned into capital in the pockets of the founders. Now, when the shares of a Company with a recognized name trade as a penny stock, you should ask the question, "If I buy this stock am I going to put capital in *my* pocket by acquiring capital that is being mistaken for smoke?" (UC)

At some point in a Company's market cycle, the price may become so cheap that purchasing shares of stock issued by the Company could be considered the purchase of a call option on the Company's net assets. The life of this option is unlimited, and its value will go to zero only upon the Company's bankruptcy. Even then, the market may ascribe value to the stock if there is any light at the end of the bankruptcy tunnel. Even as United Airlines was going into Chapter 11 its stock continued to trade above $1.50.

I. Bear market strategy for the investor

If the stocks in a particular sector have entered a bear market, as determined by technical analysis discussed in Part VI, you can protect your capital by: either selling all stock held in that sector, or purchasing additional shares at progressively lower prices in a dollar cost averaging strategy, or holding the stock in anticipation of a recovery in price.

1. *Selecting a strategy.* An investor who does not want to sell stock in the face of a bear market must be prepared to accept shrinkage in capital. If the bear market is average in length and the investor will not need the invested funds to provide a standard of living until the bear has passed, the shrinkage may be acceptable.

2. *Timely implementation of a selling strategy.* Until major stock indexes have declined twenty percent from their highs, and this may take months, the financial press will not proclaim the existence of a general bear market. Since many bear markets have not exceeded a thirty percent decline from start to finish, by the time you decide to bail out, adopting a sell all stock strategy will generally be both tardy and counter-productive (OC).

3. ***Buy the bargains.*** During a bear market even well regarded companies with good track records can fall out of bed in price on excessive volume. This is the time an astute investor will use the cash held in reserve to take a position (UC).

J. Market timing

1. ***Timing short-term reversals in the major trend.*** Moving capital entirely out of stocks into cash and then subsequently back into stocks in an effort to take advantage of short-term reversals in the major trend of the market (OC) is not a stock market operation for investors.

Observation

In the first place, identifying the turning point that marks a significant short-term reversal of the market's major trend is very difficult. In the second place, there will always be some stocks that will not participate in short-term contra moves but will keep progressing. Dumping these stocks to catch a short-term move in the opposite direction will cost you money.

2. ***Timing the sectors.*** Some investor's use managed mutual funds as their principal investment. They believe these funds will provide their capital with professional management and diversification as well as the opportunity to invest in the currently

"hottest" market sectors. If you want to try this strategy, do not go it alone. Subscribe to an investment advisory service, such as Jim Lowell's *Fidelity Investor*, that recommends or discourages the purchase of particular managed mutual funds. This publication attempts to identify the funds with the most upside potential from among Fidelity's many offerings.

Observation

Mutual funds charging no commissions on their purchase or sale, i.e., true "no load" funds, reduce the cost of investing in equities and facilitate periodically moving funds from one market sector to another. The charges imposed by "load" funds, or partial load funds can be as high as 5% of the principal on the purchase or sale of shares. Such charges must be considered in evaluating the probable return from "load" funds purchased to time market sectors.

Even if you purchase shares in "no load" funds to time market sectors, you run the risk of being a day late and a dollar short. The popularity contest that is the market of stocks can be extremely fickle in delivering long-term gains on an intermediate swing in any particular sector. The rotation in popularity among sectors will generally occur more frequently than every eighteen months.

Consider that it takes between three to six months for a sector to be recognized as currently "hot," and an equal amount of time to discover that a sector has gone cold. These verification requirements make it very difficult to find a twelve-month interstitial period when you are able to buy and sell managed mutual funds in a successful long-term sector timing strategy (OC).

3. ***Investing with the market.*** The rate of return goal for many investors is simply to match the positive performance of the market for any period of time. This market performance will be reflected in a market index such as the Dow Jones Industrial Average, the Russell 1000 or Russell 2000, the Fortune 500, Wilshire Total Market Index, Nasdaq composite or NYSE index.

   (a) ***Mutual fund products.*** One of the more popular mutual fund products developed to meet the demand for investors who wish to match market performance are index funds such as the Fidelity Spartan 500 Index Fund. The goal of this fund is to replicate the performance of the Standard and Poor's 500 Index. The Spartan has one hundred and twenty four million shares outstanding with a market capitalization of over nine billion dollars.

The purchase of a share in an index fund gives the mutual fund shareholder indirect ownership of a minute interest in the stock of all companies included in the measuring index. The number of shares of each company owned by the Fund is recalculated daily so that its portfolio replicates the market-weighted composition of that index.

(b)   *Exchange Traded Funds.* Investigations, not by the SEC but by the Attorney General of New York, Eliot Spitzer, have disclosed that during the bear market, mutual fund managers and officers engaged in frequent trading, weekly or more often, of fund shares. This may perturb (enrage?) some public investors who were limited by the mutual fund's prospectus to twice per year transactions. To enjoy a level trading field, these investors can replace their index fund shares with shares in exchange-traded stock funds (EFT). For example, shares of one widely held EFT, DIAMONDS Trust Series I, may be bought and sold daily on the American Stock Exchange. The price moves up and down in real time at approximately 10% of the Dow Jones Industrial Average.

The AMEX describes DIAMONDS as follows:

DIAMONDS represent ownership in the DIAMONDS, Trust Series I, a unit investment trust established to accumulate and hold a portfolio of the equity securities that comprise the Dow Jones Industrial Average. DIAMONDS seek investment results that, before expenses, generally correspond to the price and yield performance of the DJIA. There is no assurance that the price and yield performance of the DJIA can be fully matched.

4. ***Advice from the professor***. A highly regarded book on investing in the market of stocks, *Stocks for the Long Run*, now in its third edition, has been written by Professor Jeremy J. Siegel. His advice is very clear.

Invest the largest percentage—the core holdings of your stock portfolio—in either highly diversified mutual funds with low expense ratios, exchange-traded funds (EFTs), or indexed mutual funds. To replicate the *returns described in this book* (emphasis added), it is necessary to hold a highly diversified portfolio of stocks unless you can consistently choose stocks with superior returns, a goal very few investors have achieved. Jeremy J. Siegel, *Stocks for the Long Run*, McGraw Hill 2002, 361

What are the *returns described in this book* referred to by Professor Siegel? Here is some relevant performance data that he provides.

At the end of the 1960's bull market in 1966 the Dow Jones Industrial Average had reached the then magical level of 1000.That market was driven by the "nifty fifty" stocks; the tech stocks of that era. Fifteen years later in 1981 there had been no progress in the DJIA. In point of fact, adjusted for inflation, the overall market had actually lost 4/10 of a percent per year. Siegel, *Stocks for the Long Run*, 361.

Market peaks are typically followed by modest returns. The average inflation adjusted advance in the overall market after the peak prices of 1901, 1908, 1915, 1929, 1937, 1948 and 1968 over a ten year period was 25% or about 2% per year. Siegel, *Stocks for the Long Run*, 31.

The Professor's counsel regarding the minimal wealth-building opportunities after a major bull market has ended noted in his book is:

Of course, if investors can identify peaks and troughs in the market, they can outperform the buy-and-hold strategy that is advocated in this book. Needless to say, however, few investors can do this. Market timers may get satisfaction from having sold before the market declines but by not knowing when to reenter the market, they realize inferior returns to those investors who never try to time the market. Siegel, *Stocks for the Long Run,* 31, 32.

Observation

Index funds and EFTs became available after the financial services industry developed sufficient computer power to instantly measure price trends and build indexes for nearly any combination or permutation of stocks. An investor in individual stocks who focuses too intently on indexes, however, may overlook the reality that each stock trades in its own individual universe of supply and demand. The price of an individual stock is frequently, but not always, synchronous with the other stocks in its sector or the market as a whole. Further, there are *always stocks with superior returns available for purchase in the market of stocks.* One of the purposes of this book is to help the reader identify those stocks. You should not succumb to Professor Siegel's pessimism.

Summary Observation

Love and investing have common requirements for success. Both require passion and perspicacity.

V. Fundamental Analysis

You will discover the financial and non-financial information that will aid you in making "right time, right stock" decisions by using fundamental analysis. Fundamental analysis reveals quantitative and qualitative information that is both internal and external to a Company, i.e., arising from the Company's operations or the environment in which it does business.

A. Internal financial data

An important component of fundamental analysis is financial analysis or FA. FA is employed to measure financial data and establish financial ratios as benchmark criteria for the selection of stocks to buy or to sell short.

1. *Nuts and bolts of FA.* FA requires the computation of financial ratios and the comparison of those ratios between companies. Financial ratios include: rate of return on equity, rate of return on assets, dollars of sales per share, liquid assets to short term obligations, etc., etc. This paragraph could be expanded to a book length treatise. Indeed, the bedrock of FA is a the classic written in 1934, *Security Analysis,* (McGraw Hill, 1940) by Benjamin Graham himself, then an investment

fund manager, and David Dodd, a finance professor at Columbia University. *Security Analysis* has become the genesis of semester-long college courses on this subject. An investor does not have to enroll in a securities analysis course, however, to be exposed to the most relevant financial ratios. Many of these ratios are generally computed and presented side by side for several years in the annual report of publicly traded companies.

2. ***FA as a predictor.*** Many traders and investors who have studied the financial ratios of their target and portfolio companies have been puzzled to find that the relationship between the direction in the price of a Company's stock and the trend in its financial ratios may have little correlation (OC). This is because the financial performance of a Company determined through FA is always a one hundred percent accurate prediction *of the past* for that Company. Experienced traders and investors know that past successful financial performance of a Company is no guarantee of a higher price for its stock in the future.

Observation

FA did not prevent the "tech wreck" that began in March of 2000. Until the bottom fell out of the price of technology stocks in early 2000, their earnings had been on a roll. Students of FA in retrospect may now claim that weakness in the financial structure of many technology companies was building and revealed by their efforts prior to the collapse, but traders, and most investors as well, relied on momentum in these stocks and chose to ignore the dimly perceived financial realities. (OC).

3. *Application of financial analysis.* The occupation (and financial future) of thousands of AE security analysts is based on the following spreadsheet drill. Any analyst worthy of his credentials will practice this drill for sixty or more hours per week in studious contemplation of the stable of related stocks under his scrutiny. Moreover, the drill must be repeated quarterly or more frequently to take into account new information the analyst gathers from researching published information and interviewing management AEs.

Here is the six-step spreadsheet drill:

(i) Use FA on current Company data to predict the *future* sales and earnings of the Company over a five-year period.

(ii) Determine the present value of the earnings during that five-year period by applying an appropriate discount factor to this earnings stream.

(iii) Determine the "terminal reserve" value of the Company for the indefinite future after the five-year period. This may be done by multiplying an appropriate price to sales ratio times the projected sales for the sixth year.

(iv) Return the future terminal reserve to the present by applying an appropriate discount factor.

(v) Combine the present value determined for the five year earnings stream with the present value of the terminal reserve and divide the total by the number of shares outstanding to determine the current "true" value per share for the stock.

(vi) Compare the "true" value per share with the current market price per share to determine whether the stock is presently over or under-priced.

The end result of this number crunching is the analyst's "Buy," "Sell" or "Hold" advisory on the stock. If the market subsequently validates the analyst's decision, his judgment becomes respected, followed, and finally self-proving. But there is always the lurking question, "Does this six-step prognostication matrix require the financial analyst to be skilled at coin flipping?"

Observation

Investors and traders who do not have an accounting background, or lack the time or patience to master the complexities of FA, may believe they cannot use FA effectively. Do not let such a belief be a barrier to your success. You do not have to analyze the financial statements of your portfolio and target companies to benefit from reading these statements. As you read each Company's annual statement sent to each shareholder, the numbers will begin to speak for themselves. Growth or decline in sales will jump off the page. Changes in the number of shares of stock outstanding, earnings per share and number of shareholders will become information that you note. The equity to debt ratio, current assets to short-term debt and other financial ratios *calculated by the Company* and presented in its annual report will become old friends. In due time exposure to this quantitative data will make you more and more knowledgeable about your investments, and comparisons between your portfolio and target stocks will start to arise in your mind.

4. *The discount rate.* In determining the present true value of a stock, should the Security Analyst apply the same discount rate the future earnings of a Company whether or not it pays dividends?

Arguably, in computing the discounted cash flow value of a stock, a lower discount rate should apply if the Company pays dividends. Dividends are component of a stock's value that augments the value to the investor determined by the discounted cash flow.

B. Internal non-financial information

Fundamental analysis also requires an investor or trader to draw conclusions from current news published about a Company. This includes announcements about new products, entry into new markets, changes in management, "insider" purchases and sales of stock in the Company, mergers, etc. (UC).

Example

A Company may announce that it has engaged an investment banker to help it "maximize value" by selling or spinning off its component parts. Before the first step in this plan is taken, you can assume that management believes that the sum of the parts of the Company is worth more than the whole. Buying such a stock before the implementation of the sell off or spin off strategy may enable you to gain by acquiring the undervalued pieces.

1. ***Good news.*** There is no doubt that stock prices can react very positively to good news.

Example

"Shares of Orchid BioSciences almost doubled in trading yesterday on word that the American Association of Blood Banks had approved the company's system of genetic marking for paternity testing." *Trenton Times*, May 8, 2003.

2. *"Bad" news.* The conclusions to be drawn from internal non-financial factors particular to a Company or a particular market sector may be counter-intuitive. For example, there is an old investment adage that says, "Buy on strike news." And most importantly if the bad news barrel is almost empty, the trader or investor should see this as a reason to buy even as a stock is tanking on the latest lemon in the mouth announcement.

3. *Consider the source.* Is news being released about the Company simply to tout its stock? You must go behind the news and consider the source and the motives that may underlie its distribution. The purpose of the news may in fact be designed to get the public to act against its own best interests and for the benefit of the AE source (OC). As previously discussed, investment bank analysts, working hand in glove with the underwriting division of the same bank, have not had a reputation for objectivity in their advice to the public.

4. *Anticipate the news.* A trader can make serious money by anticipating news. For example, Altria

(formerly the Philip Morris tobacco company) appealed a multi-billion-dollar damage award. What was the likelihood of the Court of Appeals permitting a Trial Court's decision to stand that would put Altria out of business for the benefit of a few smokers? Recall that these same smokers had been warned for decades by package labels that smoking was harmful to their health. The Trial Court's decision also threatened the cash flow to all of the state governments from the tobacco settlement entered into by the industry. Traders making a logical bet on a modification of the Trial Court's position were handsomely rewarded. Altria stock advanced 25% in one day on the announcement of the Court of Appeal's decision (UC).

Now we turn from information internal to a Company derived from fundamental analysis, to information external to that company.

C. Financial factors external to the Company

Stocks do not trade in isolation from the economy and the financial trends that sweep down the halls of history.

1. *Investment alternatives.* Nowhere is Adam Smith's "Invisible Hand" more active than in allocating capital, a scarce resource, among the many competing venues for its investment. Risk and

rate of return drive the direction and quantity of the flow of capital.

Example

If Federal Reserve action or market forces cause interest rates to decline, the dividends paid on common stock and an enhanced potential for price appreciation will make common stock of a Company a more attractive investment than its fixed-interest, non-convertible debt. The number of shares of stock at the market price represented by the redemption value of a bond issued by the Company will decrease accordingly. However, if the Company cuts its common stock dividend or offers a higher interest rate on a new bond issue the ratio of the number of shares to the redemption value of the bond will increase.

Observation

Even the interrelationships illustrated in this example are not simplistic. In the market place for money, competition for capital is keen among a multiplicity of financial investments denominated in numerous currencies whose relationship is constantly changing in an unstable interest rate environment. The interaction between these variables creates a high noise level in the investment arena. Read just one issue of the Wall Street Journal cover-to-cover and you will appreciate this point. It is beyond the scope of this Book to deal seriously with any investments other than those found in the market of stocks.

2. ***Using external financial factors.*** The best strategy for the average trader or investor to take advantage of external financial factors is a Keep It Simple, Stupid (KISS) technique.

   (a) ***Follow the money.*** Are US defense expenditures heading higher under a newly elected Republican Administration? *Follow the money* and buy defense stocks. Is a bank too big for the Federal Reserve to allow it to fail? *Follow the money* and buy this stock. Are mortgage rates headed lower? *Follow the money* and buy stocks of homebuilders. Are the combination of historically low interest rates and the expansion of the money supply through deficit spending by government going to drive people to invest in hard assets? *Follow the money* and buy natural resource stocks.

   (b) ***Other follow the money KISS scenarios.*** Put together your own, *"Follow the money"* scenario to make the use of external financial factors to help grow your portfolio. But to be successful in this effort, you must be able to follow the money before it starts moving. Getting in or out before the crowd is the key to success.

Example

Warren Buffet purchased the old Northern Natural Gas Pipeline division that tumbled out of the Enron bankruptcy for $900,000,000. A KISS and follow Buffet's money strategy was to target other natural gas distribution systems selling at discounted prices. Investors or traders who followed this strategy and bought stock in firms like Williams Cos. have been richly rewarded.

3. ***Stock market as predictor.*** The Index for the Standard and Poor's 500 largest domestic companies is one component of the Index of Leading Economic Indicators because changes in stock prices typically lead the economy. This is because stock prices rise in advance of improved economic conditions and fall before a recession hits.

Observation

It has been said that, "Good times in the economy engender greed and excessive risk taking. Difficult times breed fear and excessive risk avoidance." Bank of New York, *The Leading Indicator*, Fall 2002 Do these emotions of greed and fear affect the price of stocks sufficiently to compromise the efficacy of a stock index as a leading indicator?

4. *Impending changes in GAAP.* Earnings per share drive the stock price for many companies. Generally Accepted Accounting Principles (GAAP) drive earnings. Keep an eagle eye on the frequent pronouncements of the Financial Accounting Standards Board (FASB), the American Institute of Certified Public Accountants (AICPA) and the Securities and Exchange Commission. The pontifications of these bodies come as if handed down from triple Mount Olympi in Greenwich, CN; New York, NY; and Washington DC. But laying aside the pretensions of the GAAP authorities, we still find that fallible mere mortals establish the GAAP that determines the measurement and presentation of earnings and earnings per shares for publicly traded companies.

Example

The GAAP authorities are presently scrutinizing the accounting rules for derivatives. A change in these rules forcing money center banks such as JP Morgan to recognize the heretofore hidden losses in derivative contracts would to have a significant adverse effect on these banks' earnings. Their stock prices would most certainly decline on the announcement of a

GAAP change much in advance of the reduced earnings caused by that change.

D. Non-financial factors external to the Company

Stocks also do not trade in isolation from the political, social and regulatory trends that shape our economic environment. Several of these trends are discussed in Chapters XI and XII. There is a *find the entrepreneurs* KISS technique that can help you find connections between these events and stock prices. Is the electric power industry being transformed from a regulated monopoly to a free market? *Find the entrepreneurs* who will turn this trend to their advantage. Is China being admitted to the World Trade Organization? *Find the entrepreneurs* who will turn this trend to their advantage. Is there an Internet information distribution revolution underway? *Find the entrepreneurs* who will turn this trend to their advantage. You can create a *"Find the entrepreneur"* scenario that will enable you to take advantage of external non-financial factors to grow your portfolio.

Observation

The entrepreneurs may also be looking for you with the principal goal of selling stock and not establishing a viable business. The terms, "Manager" and "Entrepreneur" do not necessarily denote congruent skills. If you can identify a good manager, such as Bill Gates, who is also an entrepreneur intent on building a business, you will have found a moneymaking combination.

E. Effect of the Internet

The Internet has greatly enhanced the opportunity for fundamental analysis. Information previously available by paid subscription is now freely accessible to everyone with a computer link to the web. If you have an account with a discount broker such as Etrade or Scottrade, even "streaming quotes" are available. These are the prices paid within the last five minutes for your portfolio or target stocks. One problem with the now ubiquitous availability of information is time. No one has the time required to functionally absorb the overwhelming amount of data pouring down the glass wires every millisecond. Extracting what is truly useful from this stream of data and leaving the dross to die in cyberspace is very difficult.

Many investors, not being up to this task, will continue to plod ahead with investments as before and rely on their independent (dependent?) CFP, CFA or other credentialed investment advisor to do the legwork for them.

Observation

Potentially, the Internet can level the playing field between AEs and individual investors. Has this potential been realized? Judging from the public's success in the market of stocks during the late great bear market the answer is "No." However, if nothing else, the Internet appears to have expanded opportunities for more workers in our society to make a living managing somebody else's money.

Summary Observation

Facts are the foundation of logic. Logic, the exercise of reason within the boundaries of objectivity and perception, must be empowered by intuition. Fundamental analysis in the market of stocks is the exercise of such logic.

VI. Technical Analysis

Among the cognoscenti who meet and size each other up at the conventions of security analysts, the "market technicians" among them comprise a very small minority. These AEs generally gather at the far end of the bar to discuss the arcane material derived from stock charts described in this chapter. The spreadsheet crowd tends to minimize the chartists' interpretative skills and considers them to be illogical bedfellows in the analysts' profession. As explained in this chapter, investors and traders, who have no professional axes to grind, should not be so quick to accept this opinion.

A. Price trends

You can determine the general trend in the price of an individual stock, or a group of stocks combined in a stock index, by daily charting on graph paper of the closing price of the stock or the index and the volume of shares traded. The longer the period of time reflected on the chart the more clearly the general trend will be revealed. A chart showing price action of a stock or a stock index for six to twelve months is normally required before you can reach a conclusion on the general trend. If the chart ultimately reveals that the general trend is up, the stock or the index is said to be in a "bull" market. If the general trend is down, the stock or the index is said to be in a "bear" market.

1. ***Bull market chart pattern.*** At its most basic, technical analysis requires the investor or trader to identify on a six to twelve month chart a rally high closing above a prior rally high, then dipping, but holding above the most recent reaction low. This pattern suggests that the trend in the price of the stock or the index is up. This is a "bull" market pattern.

2. ***Bear market chart pattern.*** On a six to twelve month chart when prices fall lower than the last decline, and then rise but fail to reach the last rally high, this pattern suggests that the trend in the price of the stock or the index is down. This is a "bear" market pattern.

3. ***Durability of trend.*** A trend in the price of a stock or an index once in place must be assumed to remain in effect until reversed by a pattern described in paragraph 1 or 2 above. A further generalization regarding the continuation of a bear market is that, "History shows that bear markets tend to last a third to half as long as their preceding bull market." Harry D. Shultz, *After a Crash Bear Market Money Making*, Datum, 1988, 66

Observation

Harry D. Shultz, editor of the *Harry Schultz International Letter*, has been reported by *Guinness Book of Records* to be the highest hourly paid consultant in the world. Shultz is a very astute student of the market of stocks. That being said, the title of his book is a bit of a misnomer. As it turned out, the 1987 crash in the stock market was not the beginning of a bear market as Shultz had anticipated. The 1929–1932 period was not repeated. In hindsight, the 1987 crash is a mere blip in the long-term bull market charts for all stock market indices.

B. Reactions against the major trend

There is always an opportunity for a trader to take advantage of the inevitable reactions against the major trend.

Reactions (whether in bull or bear markets) nearly always consume less time and are more violent than are movements in the direction of the primary trend. It is not unusual for a three-week rally in a bear market to retrace 30% to 60% of a downward swing, which may have taken many months to complete. Such a reaction presents a turn on a dime appearance; the rallies seem to spring from no visible base or area of support. Shultz, *After a Crash Bear Market Money Making*, 54.

A reaction in a bear market occurs at a time when the market has temporarily become oversold. Shultz observes that the reaction starts when AE short sellers realize that the time has come to cover their positions. Other short sellers follow the AE's lead. AE traders sense the reversal and start buying and the rally is underway. According to Shultz, the reversal is, "not a forecast of a fundamental turn but merely a technical rebound in a market that has gone too far, too fast." Shultz, *After a Crash Bear Market Money Making*, 54.

C. End of the reaction

Shultz quotes Charles Dow, the creator of the Dow Jones Industrial Average in its 1885 incarnation of ten railroads and two industrial companies, for the proposition that, "Dullness (in volume) following the peak of a bear market rally is a common danger sign." Shultz, *After a Crash Bear Market Money Making*, 54. Dow stated 1902 that, "In a bull market dullness (in volume) is generally followed by advances, in a bear market by declines."

Shultz identifies two reasons for the end of a rally; AE short selling after prices have retraced about one half of their most recent drop, and AE trader liquidation of positions purchased at a profit in the reaction. A third reason is that investors who have been on the sidelines during the bear market see the reaction as an opportunity to protect their remaining capital, and they also start to sell. As a result, the bear market rally ends.

Observation

It is easier to agree with the points made by Harry Shultz and Charles Dow than to profitably use their advice. Indeed, Shultz says, "Those who try to place an exact limit on secondary reactions are doomed to failure as certainly as the weatherman who forecasts a rainfall will be precisely one inch in 24 hours." Shultz, *After a Crash Bear Market Money Making*, 58.

D. Chart reading

The general rules stated above must be translated into useful guidance with respect to individual stocks. To this end, the following chart reading guidelines have proven helpful. The starting point is to recognize that stock price charts always reveal the history of price and volume movements in a stock, and in some cases the past may indeed be prologue.

1. *Eroding price trend.* Where the chart pattern for a stock shows a steadily eroding price over a period of time, it is a certainty that the remaining investors who have become disenchanted with that stock will diminish in numbers. At some point the supply of sellers who are investors will have become exhausted. And if these sellers are exhausted how

long can AE short sellers continue to maintain their enthusiasm? As the bear market in a stock proceeds, strong and steady hands hold a greater and greater percentage of the outstanding shares.

2. *Base building.* When the erosion in the price of a stock levels out into a flat trajectory, on reduced and below normal volume, a base is being built through the accumulation of stock by astute investors and traders. It is from this base, and after the principal bad news on the Company has been disseminated, that the price of its shares may rise like a Phoenix from the ashes. Frequently, the signal for a turn in price is a fundamental factor such as a *change in the management* of the Company or *an infusion of cash* from a cooperative lender or investor, or *an unexpectedly positive earnings report.* There will be large economic rewards if you can appreciate the significance such events (UC) before the AEs wake up and *act on the courage of your convictions to buy the stock when others remain on the sidelines.*

3. *Chart action points.* Traders will not tie up their capital in a waiting game that is a patient base building strategy. Most will use charts that show a 10 or 20 day moving average price line and buy when a stock breaks significantly above the line on expanding volume and then retreats to the line and holds. Other traders will try to spot a "Head and Shoulders" pattern that will identify short

sale candidates as they pitch off the right shoulder into the abyss. And nearly all AEs who use technical analysis even as a secondary tool will consider the following price patterns as propitious for taking action:

(a) **_Signal to purchase_** The trader will connect the bottom price points of declines of a stock with a ascending price in the mind's eye or with a straight edge. If fundamental analysis reveals positive facts about the Company, the trader will buy on a downward reaction in the price of the stock that turns upward at that line.

(b) **_Signal to sell short_** The trader will connect the top price points of advances of a stock with a descending price in the mind's eye or with a straight edge. If fundamental analysis reveals negative facts about the Company, the trader will sell short on an upward reaction in the price of the stock that turns downward at that line.

Observation

A stock chart will always reveal the history of the price of a stock or market index. This information should raise the question, "How does the current price of a stock compares to its historical price." If past earnings and prospects were equal to the present, but the previous price was much higher, the stock may be a candidate for purchase. In other words your study of a stock's price and trading volume chart should be accompanied by fundamental analysis as well. However, to rely solely upon a pattern in the price and volume chart of a stock to predict its future price is very problematical. Many patterns abort before completion. And for the patterns that are clearly completed, post-pattern prices frequently are not what the chartists anticipated. If the majority of investors or traders *know* that a particular chart pattern will produce a certain future result, then that result will occur too infrequently to permit consistent moneymaking.

E. The equilibrium price

The equilibrium price for any stock at any point in time is the price at which the buying pressure and the selling pressure are equal and offsetting. A shortfall in the pressure on either side will move the price out of equilibrium and in that direction. As previously mentioned, much of the selling pressure for many widely held stocks comes from the artificial supply of loaned stock sold by short sellers. It should be no surprise that when the short sellers stop selling and start to cover their shorts, the price of a stock or an index can re-price to a new and much higher equilibrium price very quickly (OC). How quickly? As with charitable giving and other financial events, the

20/80 rule is applicable to stocks. You will find that 80% of the movement in the price of a stock between its high and its low during the year will occur on 20% or fewer of all trading days. Most of the time the equilibrium price of a stock is in a relatively narrow range. To expand upon the tuning fork analogy discussed earlier, most stocks are waiting to be struck.

1. *Using the equilibrium price.* When a stock takes off like a shot, the question is, "What will be the next equilibrium price?" This price will reflect a pullback from a dramatic upward move. Selling just before the pullback will optimize a trader's profits but it is axiomatic that this is a price point known with certainty only in retrospect. It is possible, however, to sell after the chart patterns reveal a new equilibrium price (UC). Selling on the way up before the charts reveal this price can have a high opportunity cost. This is called, "Not letting your profits run."

2. *Switch and lose trades.* Many traders and even investors frequently compound the error of selling before the new equilibrium price is established and then shifting the small profit on the trade into another stock. This compounding strategy will backfire if the replacement stock experiences a shortfall in buying pressure and drops rather than advances in price. The gains made in the first proper stock selection are thus

consumed in the second improper stock selection. Nothing is more frustrating to a trader than selling too early, switching into a loser, and then watching the price of the original winning stock continue to increase (OC).

F. Cycles

There are certain cycle theory experts who flatly say that the past predicts and may therefore control the future. For example, a famous commodity trader and purveyor of trading advice, W.D. Gann, concluded after research in the Astor library in England that commodity price cycles repeat every sixty years come hell or high water. Gann's students have applied his theories to the market of stocks with sporadic success.

Observation

For what it is worth, the pattern and up move of the 2003 Dow Jones Industrial Average had an eerie resemblance to the pattern and up move of the 1943 Dow Jones Industrial Average.

Robert Prechter, a strong advocate of the validity of market cycles, publishes *The Elliot Wave Theorist*. His theories are based on the market timing cycles of R.N. Elliot. Prechter's success in the 1980's is legendary, but the wave theory he relied upon predicted a crash in the 1990's instead of the towering bull market that actually occurred.

Another important (if not as well known) proponent of market cycles is the Russian economist Nikolai Kondratieff. His students are currently projecting the imminent arrival of a "Kondratieff winter" in which the world economy, in the inescapable grip of a sixty to seventy year major cycle, is inexorably crushed by the Fates.

G. Technical resources—*TAST*

The Bible for students of technical analysis is the previously cited book, *Technical Analysis of Stock Trends*, referred to here as *TAST*. The bottom line of this formidable and lengthy tome stated on page 1 of the Preface is, "Chart formations are the language of the market." The implication is that if you learn the language of chart formations (patterns) as taught in *TAST*, you can master the market of stocks.

1. ***TAST Editors*** *TAST* was originally published in 1948 by co-authors Robert D. Edwards and John McGee. After the second edition of *TAST* was released in 1951, Edwards dropped his pen. John McGee plowed ahead solo with the project until 1966 through three more editions. However, during the remaining 21 years of his life McGee turned the task of revising the book over to others while he edited and published the *Technical Stock Advisory Service*, an investment newsletter dedicated to trading the market by means of technical chart patterns. During the post *TAST*

period, McGee also found time to write a book, *The General Semantics of Wall Street* initially published in 1958 and subsequently reissued under the title, *Winning the Mental Game on Wall Street,* which was published by St. Lucie Press in 2000.

2. ***Permanency of teaching.*** The current eighth edition (2001) of *TAST* offers new material on portfolio management and risk analysis. However, the editor, W.H.C. Bassetti, is clear in his defense of the insights of the original authors, "Have any new chart patterns (that is to say, changes in human behavior and character) emerged since the 5th edition? Not to my knowledge..." Edwards and McGee, *TAST*, 3

3. ***Reliance on Dow Jones Industrial Average questioned.*** Mr. Bassetti, however, calls into question the reliance on the charts of the Dow Jones Industrial Average of 30 industrial stocks (DJIA) or the Dow Jones Rails (Transportation Index) as a way to predict market behavior. He readily acknowledges that the DJIA may be in a reversal of a previously established bull or bear market while the primary trend is still firmly established in other indexes such as the Nasdaq or the Standard and Poor's 500. Bassetti's conclusion is that for the Edwards and McGee approach of using chart patterns to accurately predict overall

future market direction, a *composite index* would have to be created that included appropriate elements of not only the DJIA, but also the Nasdaq and the S&P 500. Edwards and McGee *TAST*, 24. No such composite index exists, of course, because the technical problems in properly selecting and weighting the stocks to be included in such an index are formidable.

Observation

In the absence of a composite index, the most certain application of technical analysis would be limited to the chart user's investment in the stocks of the DJIA or the Dow Jones Transportation Average. Then the task is to find a predictive technical chart pattern in that average before the move in price signaled by the pattern has already occurred. Only a technician intrepid enough to predict the future for a particular stock from its chart pattern without concern for the direction of the market would not be troubled by the lack of an appropriately composite market index.

H. Technical resources—charts and other tools

There are many excellent services available for use in technical analysis such as those found at: *dailygraphs.com, bigcharts.com, stockcharts.com, dailystocks.com, litwik.com* (candlestick charts), *magiccharts.com* (point and figure charts), *stocks.tradingcharts.com, incrediblecharts.com* (charting software), *chartpatterns.com* (technical patterns illustrated), and *howamazing.com* (stock screening software). The investor or trader who is interested in pursuing technical analysis will not have to personally draw pen and pencil charts. The graph paper method mentioned at the outset of this Chapter was to illustrate the concept. This method is long since outdated. Computer generated stock charts are available from the sources cited above and other suppliers.

Observation

Many investors and traders who have relied upon chart reading to the exclusion of fundamental analysis have concluded that using charts to predict stock prices is the modern day equivalent of casting and reading rune sticks or tarot cards. The messages received from the study of charts are enigmatic at best. The early departure of both Edwards and McGee from their job as the authors and editors of *TAST* suggest they may have doubted the certainty of this stock price prediction methodology. It is abundantly clear that news about a Company and salient events in the economy are usually associated with any noticeable move in the price of the stock or in a market index. News and events are usually fairly contemporaneous with stock price moves. A trader or investor who applies time and talent to anticipating news will gain more profits than spending the same amount of time trying to divine stock chart patterns and their implications (UC).

Summary Observation

Be kind to your web-footed friends. That duck may indeed be somebody's mother. While the use of stock charts is not a panacea, technical analysis and its practitioners are able to provide helpful insights and support that will nurture your investing and trading decisions.

VII. Stock Selection

The message of the previous two chapters is that a successful trader or investor is a generalist who must use both fundamental and technical analysis without being a slave to either system. An investor should also be a realist. My Uncle Walt said about people, "You must take a person the way he is and not the way you wish him to be." This chapter suggests that Uncle Walt's advice is equally applicable to stocks.

A. Building your portfolio

You should identify stocks with recognized names that you conclude are under-priced by your fundamental analysis and appear oversold from a review of their chart, i.e. the price is trending up but remains well below its apparent resistance level. The investor can purchase such a stock with a valid expectation of success. Reserve some funds so that you can add to your investment if the stock you have purchased declines in price (UC). If none of your target stocks wears the "under-priced and oversold" labels, then expand your watch list. Do not chase any stock. Hold the stocks you have purchased before selling them until the reasons for your purchase no longer apply (UC).

B. Key questions

In studying the trees of this Book, don't forget that the forest is found in two elemental questions. "Is this stock the right stock?" and, "Is this time the right time to buy?"

1. *Cardinal rule.* The questions state the cardinal rule for investors or traders: on the long side *you make your money on a stock when you buy*, i.e., you must buy the right stock at the right time. Enabling you to obey the "right stock, right time" rule has been the unstated goal of this Book. At best, the failure to obey this rule will cause your capital to stagnate and diminish in a dead end investment, sometimes for years. At worst, your capital will disappear if the stock you purchase is 180 degrees off the mark as in the case of now bankrupt companies like K-Mart (inept management) or World-Com (dishonest management) (OC).

2. *Looking backward.* Most investors frequently do not observe the "right stock right time rule." Investing in last year's winners is one reason. "Just three companies that appeared on our last year's Bloomberg's 100 are back." "The Bloomberg 100" (annual review of year's best performing stocks) *Personal Finance*, February 2003, 43 (OC).

3. *Looking at current results.* When higher earnings (or increased sales for unprofitable companies) are announced at the time the Company's quarterly financial statements are released, this

may be news that strikes the stock. But you must be careful. Did the stock's price advance prior to the announcement already discount the effect of that news? If so, the apogee of the current move may have been reached before the earnings news ever became public.

Observation

When a Company's management gets on the horn to discuss the most recent quarter's financial results, its "guidance" on earnings' prospects for future quarters generally has more impact on the price action of a stock than the earnings reported for the quarter just past. This guidance is scrutinized, parsed and analyzed by the AEs of that Company's stock like economists study the comments of Federal Reserve Chairman Alan Greenspan before a Congressional Committee. Is management's guidance phrased optimistically or is there a mixed message buried in the verbiage?

C. Future earnings as a selection criteria

Stock selection must take into account the economic theory that the price of a share of stock at any point in time reflects the discounted present value of the Company's future free cash flow. This was illustrated in Chapter V in the discussion of the spreadsheet drill performed by financial analysts. The most important component of the cash flow is *earnings per outstanding share of stock or "EPS."* The outstanding shares are comprised of shares already issued plus shares that may be issued upon the exercise of employee stock options that would currently yield income to the option holders, i.e., "in the money options." EPS divided into the current market price of a stock yields the price earnings (PE) ratio. Measuring the earnings in EPS so that the PE can be properly computed raises several complex issues.

1. ***GAAP earnings.*** Under SEC rules a public Company is required to report earnings quarterly and annually as determined in accordance with Generally Accepted Accounting Principles (GAAP). The GAAP earnings must be shown in financial statements audited in accordance with Generally Accepted Auditing Standards (GAAS). But to paraphrase the conclusion reached by the pigs in George Orwell's classic book, *1984,* all GAAP earnings are desirable but some GAAP earnings are more desirable than other GAAP earnings.

2. ***"Quality" of earnings.*** Should "earnings" of a Company that include a surplus locked up in a pension plan be given the same weight by an investor as earnings of another Company derived solely from net profits on sales? Which type of earnings can be used to pay dividends, retire debt or buy back stock to enhance shareholder returns? The quantity of

earnings is important but no less so is the "quality" of those earnings. For example, how many components of the Company's statements of consolidated cash flows offset reported earnings? What portion of the reported EPS is a one-time event? How are earnings being influenced upward or downward by "accounting adjustments" rooted in some arcane technical bulletin issued by the Financial Accounting Standards Board? Are transactions of a type that are infrequently repeated on an annual basis segregated from operating earnings on the Company's income statement? These transactions include expenses and income related to "restructuring" the Company.

Observation

The FASB gurus of the accounting profession are presently reviewing the whole concept of the "rule based" creation of corporate balance sheet and income statement numbers. GAAP has become a very legalistic method of measuring earnings by means of the application of hundreds of black letter rules issued by the FASB and the SEC and hundreds of additional interpretations by the AICPA applicable to specific financial statement line items. The departure of firms from the accounting profession such as the late Arthur Anderson CPA's, who played the rule based measure of earnings game to the hilt, may hasten the adoption of the British standard of a more simple requirement of a "true and fair" presentation of financial data in the Company's financial statements. There is a debate at the highest levels of the accounting profession over whether the US should move toward such a "Principles" based rather than a "Rules" based GAAP.

3. **_Earnings computed under Industry Accounting Guidelines (IAG)._** Should the sale of fixed assets be taken into operating earnings or considered an extraordinary item? The answer would seem obvious, but not so. For 1999, the year prior to the California power industry deregulation fiasco, Edison International (EIX), a major California electric utility, reported EPS that were largely the result of the sale of its power plants. The electric generating Industry Accounting Guidelines permitted this treatment. Perhaps this anomalous rule had as much to do as deregulation with subsequent collapse in the price of an EIX share from over $30.00 to a low of just over $6.00. The Company had no earnings from actual operations even prior to deregulation. In your review of a Company's financial statements it is important to identify and understand IAG rules that affect that Company's earnings.

4. ***Earnings computed under International Accounting Standards (IAS).*** If you invest in American Depository Receipts in stocks of foreign companies you will receive annual financial statements that present earnings computed under both GAAP and International Accounting Standards (IAS). Companies resident in the countries of the European Union are required to use IAS in compiling their financial statements.

D. Revenue from operations

Stocks with the greatest potential for appreciation in price are in companies whose goods or services have an *accelerating sales growth curve.* If the market for the goods or services sold by a particular Company is expanding, prices for the Company's output will be firm and the effect of competition on pricing power limited. Growth in the Company's EPS depends only upon management's ability to exploit an expanding market and to control costs. If competent, stock option rewarded management rises to this task, the resulting growth in current earnings will stimulate investors to overpay for future earnings and the PE will stretch out like an accordion.

1. ***Importance of growth in sales.*** Actual or potential growth in a company's sales is a key determinant of growth in the price of its stock. An investment advisory service with an excellent track record over many years, the *Value Line Report*, puts dollars of sales per share as the first line of data on every stock report it issues. Also, to see how sales can be used as a tool in security analysis read, *What Works on Wall Street*, James P. O'Shaughnessy McGraw Hill

(1997) or *Super Stocks*, Kenneth L. Fisher, Dow Jones Irwin (1984). (UC)

In writing his book, O'Shaugnessy performed Herculean statistical work on 10,000 individual companies over a fifty-year period to show that the stocks with the lowest price to sales ratios (P/S) performed the best. The P/S ratio is computed by dividing the current market price of a stock by the dollars of sales per share. The stock of companies trading at a P/S of under two had the best prospects for appreciation, while stocks with a P/S of three or more had much less potential.

Observation

"Sales" dollars cannot always be taken at face value. The sales of Duke Energy (DUK) in 1999 tripled from the prior year due to its frenetic electricity trading. Before the market recognized that the Company's mark to market paper earnings were just as mythical as its sales, the price of a share of DUK stock hit $55.00. But after the charade became known, DUK shares lost two thirds of this value. Management has subsequently abandoned energy trading and reported sales in DUK's financial statements have returned to real numbers.

2. *The technology stock fiasco.* Can companies that produce high tech capital goods or the components

for such goods deliver on a promise of consistent sales growth? The obvious answer from the collapse in the stock prices of technology companies during the bear market is a resounding, "No." The products of companies in the technology stock category have an attenuated life cycle. Therefore, it is a tautology that the PE ratio of these stocks must reflect the ever-present risk that next year's sales will collapse. During the 1990's bull market in technology stocks, investors ignored this fact. They learned too late in the game that the high-flying winners acquired during the boom were in reality clipped-wing turkeys.

3. ***Declining revenues*** Declining revenue from operations reported in a Company's quarterly financial statements is a marker that a trader will use to identify target stocks for short selling.

E. A Company's cash flow

The current cash flow from a Company's operations is another useful tool that will aid in stock selection. Accounting rules can be adopted that massage earnings or pump up "operating profits". Aside from the sale of receivables to convert this current asset to cash, a Company's cash flow from operations is not so easily improved by decisions made under the green eyeshade. An investor who focuses attention on the cash flow from operations per share reported by a Company may have a better tool for evaluating its stock than the Company's EPS.

1. ***King Cash Ratio.*** The Motley Fool is an organization dedicated to iconoclastic security analysis. It was a voice crying in the wilderness against the excesses of the boom in technology stocks during the 1990's. The Fool's King Cash Ratio combines both cash flow and sales. The numerator of the ratio is the operating cash flow of the Company minus capital improvements. The denominator of the ratio is dollars of sales. The larger the fraction represented by this ratio the more solid the Company. The smaller the fraction the weaker the Company. The Fool's King Cash Ratio answers the question, "From each dollar of sales how much cash is generated for the Company?"

2. ***Cash Flow from financing activities.*** GAAP requires all public companies to present consolidated statements of cash flows as part of their financial statements. But you should not focus simply on the bottom line increase or decrease in cash on this statement. GAAP requires that this number include cash flow from financing activities. This is a separate category of transactions and includes such items as changes in the Company's debt levels and proceeds from the sale or cash applied to the repurchase of its stock. Cash flow from financing activities has little to do

with management's effectiveness in generating cash from operating the business.

F. Identify moving sectors

In selecting stocks to purchase or to sell short, the investor or trader must be aware that at any point in time buying or selling pressure tends to focus on stocks in one or more specific market sectors.

1. *Look forward not backward.* The investor, who spots an impending up-trend in the sales of a sector before that trend becomes established, and invests in that sector, will experience capital growth. The investor, who spots an impending downtrend in the sales of a sector before that trend becomes established, and disinvests in that sector, will preserve capital. Last year's winning sector is frequently old news and this year's yawner. Stocks are like steak. Don't let the stock or the steak become well done before in(g/v)esting.

2. *Spot the laggards.* Identify the moving stock sectors and identify the stagnant stocks. Those stocks with the best numbers determined by fundamental analysis are the first ones to move, but sooner or later, "All the girls dance."

3. **Fashions change.** Stocks compete with each other in a popularity contest. In investments, as in women's clothing, fashion trends strongly influence buyer behavior. And as with women's cloth-

ing, stock sectors come into fashion and go out of fashion with regularity. Don't get caught buying last year's goods in the market of stocks even if the price is marked down.

G. Look in your backyard

Since your time and patience for stock research is limited, it is a good practice to look for target stocks among familiar businesses such as your bank, favorite restaurant, or brand name consumer products used in your household, etc. (UC).

Example

Peter Lynch, the investment guru who made outsized gains for investors in the Fidelity Magellan Fund during the 1980's even before the bull market of the 1990's, recounts his experience with L'eggs, the nylon stockings package that put the Hanes Corporation at the top of the charts. "I didn't find L'eggs in my research, she (Carolyn, his wife) found it by going to the grocery store." Peter Lynch, *One Up on Wall Street* Simon & Schuster, 2000, 36.

H. Management

Top-flight managers of business and premier professional athletes share the upper rung of compensation in the US economy for their services. The reason is simple. The members of each group make their team a winner. And if the corporate team is a winner, shareholders will be rewarded. The importance of management to the selection of your target stocks is seen in the large number of lead articles featuring managers of companies in well-known financial periodicals such as *Fortune* and *Business Week*. This editorial policy is not intended to recruit the readers of *People* to these business publications.

Observation

From the bygone days of Henry Ford and Walter Chrysler to the more recent management exploits of Jack Welch, the unique contribution of creative, charismatic and motivating management to the profitability of a Company cannot be denied. In the first instance, you should look for visionary and in-charge top management in each Company in which you choose to invest. In addition, you should require that a Company's top and second level management both own a significant amount of stock in the Company. Avoid investing in a Company where management is not in the game but sits on the sidelines with a pocket full of stock options. For a masterful treatise demonstrating the benefits of good management for shareholders see *Good to Great,* Jim Collins, Harper Business (2001)

I. Value of a share of stock

What is the value of a share of stock? This value is not only in the eye of the beholder. The closing prices for the shares of publicly traded companies are published in the stock tables of many daily general and financial newspapers such as *Barron's*, the *Investor's Business Daily* and the *Wall Street Journal*. The published price each day represents a consensus of opinion on the value of the stock of those persons who traded it on that day. Accompanying the price there is usually a display of dividends paid per share and the stock's price-earning ratio (PE). Investors are interested in these data as bearing on the value of the stock.

Some investors consider the PE to state a payback period. For example, a PE of 10 means that the value of the stock will be earned before taxes by the Company in ten years. Others consider the PE to be a rate of return measure. To these investors a PE of 10 means a ten percent rate of return on their stock, albeit the return is locked up in the Company. A lower PE indicates a shorter payback period or a higher rate of return. These attributes might make the stock more attractive to some investors. On the other hand, investors looking for cash in the pocket will emphasize dividends. Professor Siegel, who is clearly in this camp, goes so far as to say, "Note that the price of the stock is always equal to the present value of all future dividends and not the present value of future earnings." Jeremy J. Siegel, *Stocks for the Long Run*, 93. Is this statement true? Very close to one half of all publicly traded stocks have no earnings in any given year, and among the companies that do have earnings, dividend-payers are in the minority.

How can it be explained that thousands of stocks trading at prices far in excess of zero display the double anomaly of no earnings and no dividends? One reason is that AE traders who buy on the basis of momentum support these prices. The second reason is that the value ascribed to a share of stock by many, perhaps even a majority, of investors is based on their perception of the *present value of growth opportunities* (PVGO). This is the promise that determines what a share of stock is worth for a large number of companies. Stocks in the technology sector are typically priced on a PVGO basis by investors who are aware of the nifty changes technology is bringing to their daily lives.

Observation

In a bull market, the high PE of a stock issued by a Company paying no dividends is considered by some to be a reason for investors to be optimistic about growth opportunities. They believe the high PE reflects the opinion of other buyers of the stock that earnings will increase in the future. These optimistic investors further identify the lack of dividends with management's intention to finance growth without incurring debt. But when the future arrives and the AE traders are selling short, if the Company's earnings do not increase while its debt does, bitter is the cup for investors who did not foresee the demise of the promise on which they had based their decisions to buy such a stock.

J. The decision point

The analytical stock selection rules discussed above can be helpful, but experience in making investments and intuition may be equally more reliable guides to help an investor reach a final decision on whether to buy or sell a stock.

1. ***Pay attention to your intuition.*** Pay attention to the ideas formed in your mind over several days or weeks and, as a litmus test, remain there until resolved by action or an adamant dismissal. Good investment decisions are not the result of instant illumination or disillusionment. There is a necessary gestation period for any valid wealth building idea to come into being (UC).

2. ***Get there first.*** Your intuitive thoughts or "hunches" will usually predate the necessarily more cautious timing of an investment advisor who waits until financial results of the Company are in the can if not already published before making a recommendation to buy or sell its stock. The investor's goal should be to arrive at a decision

point in advance of the AEs who invariably have ways to ferret out pertinent information before it is filed with the Securities and Exchange Commission. The analyst AEs at organizations such as First Call, Standard and Poor's, Value Line, or Thomson's Financial Services, live or die on their earnings predictions.

3. *Make comparisons.* Test your intuition by making a comparison between the opportunity for gain in the target stock you decided to buy and the ones left on the shelf. Did the stock you select optimize your investment or trading success? (UC) You can take this self-examination to another level by using financial analysis to derive benchmark ratios such as return on equity, annualized growth in sales, the King Cash ratio, etc. to help you see objectively how the stock you chose compares with other stocks you did not purchase.

Summary Observation

Success in investing is optimized by the selection of stocks currently under-priced because their promise of future growth is recognized by the few and ignored by many.

VIII. Timing the Purchase or Sale

Timing the purchase or sale of a stock is a pivotal issue that must be correctly resolved for a trader or investor to realize consistent profits.

A. Tracking individual stocks vs. the market

It is important to recognize that a stock may end its own bull market and start a bear market move, or vice versa, before any index reveals a change in the group's or the market's direction. When the AEs believe a particular stock has put in its low price in the current price cycle, and act on that belief, positive things happen quickly to the price of that stock. Likewise, when the AEs believe that a stock has reached its high in the current price cycle and act on that belief, negative things happen quickly to the price of that stock.

B. The bottom

How low can the price of a stock go? Stock issued by even the most well known companies can be driven down to and even well below net book value. This is true in spades for a Company with assets that have a large "soft" component such as goodwill or other intangible non-financial assets.

1. ***Irrational selling.*** The stock sales that drive a Company's share price inexorably downward are frequently initiated by AE put buyers and short sellers on a bear raid augmented by weak hands holders dumping in fear. Companies with widely held stock announcing bad news are especially vulnerable to being the poster children of a bear market. The greater the number of shareholders the greater the potential fear driven weak hands selling that leads to irrational price declines (OC).

2. ***Rational selling.*** However, many plunging stocks are cheap for a reason other than the irrational behavior of erstwhile investors and the connivance of AEs. Frequently, the reason for the price decline is a financial disaster in the making. Creditors can put an illiquid borrower into bankruptcy and wipe out the equity holders with demands for payment of debt. Some stocks go down and out for this reason. It takes perceptive financial analysis to discover if bankruptcy is a reasonable probability for a target stock with a recognized name and a very low price.

Observation

Creditors are kind to some companies and unkind to others. K-Mart reported two losing quarters and its creditors who had imposed onerous debt covenants pulled the bankruptcy plug. Amazon ran a river of red ink for years and its creditors did nothing. Perhaps it was because K-Mart was unlucky enough to have had equity in appreciated real estate all over the US while Amazon conducts its dot-com business from a few leased warehouses.

3. *Shorting on the way to the bottom.* A stock under selling pressure because of repeated quarterly failures to meet earnings expectations established by Wall Street AE analysts is a sitting duck for AE short sales. No one ever asks whether or not the AE analysts' earnings expectations were just a tad high. The goal is to make money on the stock while it is in free fall due to panicky selling by its investors. The trashing of individual stocks occurs every day in the market of stocks. Short sellers who pick up the trash reap rich rewards.

4. *Finding the bottom.* When a plunging stock finally goes no lower, this usually results because of two factors. First, investors and AEs who are short sellers believe that nearly all of the bad news about the Company has been disclosed. Second, these market players consider the sum of the parts of the Company to be worth more than the whole. In other words if management called in the auctioneer, the components of the business could be sold for more than the market capitalization determined by the depressed price for its

shares. But more than the perception of a potential liquidating value is required to attract buyers back to a stock after its price has been decimated. The buyers must believe that the shrinkage in liquidating value has ended.

5. ***Bounce off the bottom.*** It is a beautiful thing to observe the management of a Company, whose stock has dropped like a stone, taking decisive action to preserve the Company's liquidating value and their jobs. These actions may be closing plants or even whole divisions, selling assets, and laying off employees wholesale, perhaps even including some of the management cadre. The realization by investors, and AE long traders and short sellers that the erosion in liquidating value has been stopped or even reversed by managements' actions will result in the most profitable period in the price cycle for a stock. This is the heralded "bounce off the bottom."

Observation

If the management's actions stick and the Company returns to profitability, the bounce will produce a new and much higher equilibrium price. Investors or traders who took notice of management's actions, correctly predicted the effects on Company fortunes, and acted on the courage of their convictions to buy the stock when it was dirt cheap, will do very well on their investment (UC).

Example

The most profitable bounce off the bottom of a name stock for all of the above reasons in the bull market that began in 2003 has been the dramatic rise in price of Corning from $1.10 at the nadir of its fortunes in 2002 during the late great bear market to over $11.00 (October 2003) as this is written.

6. *Magnitude of the bounce.* How far will the bounce carry? If the low price reached by the stock was a dollar or less, the bounce to an equilibrium price could well be three to five times or more times that low. A cursory review of the highs and lows in stock prices for any given year will reveal any number of stocks that have appreciated 1 to 5 times. A review of the chart on many stocks reveals that the descent to the bottom started with a waterfall drop due to irrational selling coupled with specialist inaction and AE short selling. The starting point of that waterfall drop is the most probable stopping point for the initial bounce off the bottom so that this level will be at the upper end of an oscillation in price for the stock.

    A stock that has moved to a multiple of its low may get ahead of the fundamentals of the

Company. It could be a candidate for short sale rather than purchase after the bounce no matter how good the current news.

As the tree grows toward the sky the attention of many AEs is attracted. These folks start to trade the issue in ever-greater volume.

Example

Sirius, one of the two companies granted a license by the Federal Communications Commission to operate satellite radio service (XMSR is the other) went public in March 2000 at $40.00 per share. After a modest rise in price to $60.00 per share the bottom fell out of the stock. The final denouement came in 2003 after the bond holders had agreed to exchange $800M in debentures for Sirius stock at $1.20 per share. Apparently many of the new shareholders found owning a penny stock incompatible with their risk tolerance and they sold out. The price of Sirius collapsed to 41 cents per share.

But this price did not last for long. Sirius' predictable, and nearly vertical, ensuing bounce off the bottom was triggered by several positive news items. In three months the price had multiplied over five times to $2.35, and the trading volume had swelled to as much as 250,000,000 shares per day or one fourth of the shares issued and outstanding! According to Eric Hellweg, CNN/Money contributing columnist, as reported on June 9, 2003 on the AOL Personal Finance page, there were two principal reasons for such a large volume of transactions in Sirius' stock.

"First, most institutional investors don't traffic in stocks that trade for less than $5. This realm is dominated by day traders and hedge funds, most of which are heavy-volume traders and are in and out of positions in a day or a week. Second, and harder to quantify, is the speculative frenzy surrounding this stock.... Many believe that it could be a major media force in a few years—and want to get in early."

Observation

To Hellweg's explanation I would add a third reason for the high volume of shares traded. Major brokerage houses will act as a principal in low priced stocks when their customer is an investor who is accumulating shares on a buy at market instruction. This doubles the number of shares traded for the investor to acquire the stock. The first sale is from seller to broker. The second sale is from broker to investor. Acting as principal also gives the broker an opportunity to convert the spread between the bid and asked price into bonus revenue which is in addition to the double commission already earned, i.e., the seller's commission and the buyer's commission.

7. ***Recommendations after the bounce.*** The financial information community generally casts a blind eye to bounce off the bottom opportunities. AE analysts tend to play it safe and base their recos on actual results or published favorable news. This conservative posture would seem quixotic when compared to the enthusiasm many AEs displayed for the hundreds of IPOs sold during the 1990's to the public solely on a pie in the sky pan business plan. As an individual trader or investor, you will generally have to recognize bounce off the bottom opportunities by your own devices. If you wait for the financial advisors to speak up about these stocks, you will miss the gravy.

C. The top

A well-known stock market adage is, "Let your profits run and cut your losses." In attempting to apply this rule, an investor soon realizes that the end of a bull market phase in the market as a whole or for an individual stock is easy to identify only in retrospect. And the trader realizes that even intermediate price tops are also very difficult to identify except in retrospect. While a bell is rung each day to mark the end of trading on the New York Stock Exchange, nobody rings a bell announcing that it is time to sell a stock. But there are signals. Market tops come at a price point where the supply begins to overwhelm the demand for an individual stock or a group of stocks. The end of the line for price advances characteristically comes when volume grows but the stock can eke out only meager gains compared to its past ebullience.

D. Weak hands shareholders

What causes supply to overwhelm demand? To answer this question we must ask another question. What are the sources of supply for any particular stock? The sources of supply that can potentially overwhelm demand originate in weak hands, i.e., hands with a seller's motivation. The following is a partial list of weak hands shareholders.

1. *Appointed Experts.* AE traders holding a long position in a stock will sell on a dime to realize a short-term trading profit of sometimes even less than that small coin. Stocks that are heavily infested by such AEs will churn through large volume and go nowhere. The large numbers of AEs who are short sellers are also a significant component of the weak hands shareholders.

Observation

Think about short selling for a moment. Shares of stock in a brokerage account can be loaned out by the street name repository for the shares such as Cede and Co., sold by short sellers back to investors who in turn have these shares deposited in street account only to be loaned out again to facilitate another round of short selling. This circular phenomenon can be used by AEs to cause the number of shares sold into the market to greatly exceed the number that would otherwise be available for sale by investors. When buyers have withdrawn from the marketplace, the marginal effect on the price of a stock from this artificially created supply can be huge.

This is why AE short sales at strategic times can break down forward momentum in a stock and cause a rout in its price to occur on surprisingly small volume. This may be compared to the large volume of purchases that nearly always is required to push the price of a stock up.

2. *Heirs.* Shareholders who inherit stock patiently held for the long term by their forbearers are usually weak hands holders. The stepped-up basis at death for assets permitted under current law until 2010 is an opportunity to diversify an inherited portfolio without a tax cost. The motivation to sell is overpowering for estates that must pay Federal and state death taxes. The supply of stock held by estates and heirs with a strong motivation to sell during any given year will affect stock

prices adversely for a large but unknown number of public companies.

This situation has created strong political pressure for Congress to eliminate the Federal estate tax entirely. Indeed, this happy event is scheduled to occur in 2010. The trade-off, however, is that the decedent's tax basis in assets of over 1.3M will be carried over to the decedent's heirs. A broader base of taxpayers is thereby being relied upon for capital gains tax to replace the revenue lost by the repeal of the estate tax on the wealthy. If carryover basis for inherited assets replaces the estate tax, the weak hands motivation to sell inherited stock disappears. This change in tax policy will reduce the supply of stock upon the death of a shareholder.

Observation

But keep the champagne corked. The Federal estate tax will come roaring back in 2011 with the exemption reduced from 3.5M in 2009 to $675,000 unless Congress acts to make the repeal permanent. If President Bush is re-elected for a second term and has a Republican-controlled Congress, repeal of the Federal estate tax is almost a certainty. If he has a Democrat-controlled Congress no action on the estate tax will be taken until after the 2008 Presidential elections.

3. ***Public Charities.*** The contribution deduction allowed for the paper profits in appreciated stock is an incentive for tax-deductible gifts to public charities in the form of stock rather than cash. Public charities receiving gifts or bequests of appreciated stock usually unload it quickly in order to invest more conservatively and earn a larger current income.

4. ***Private Foundations.*** A private *non-operating foundation* is a charity that is required under the rules of the Internal Revenue Code to distribute at least five percent of the average value of its asset base of the prior year to public charities. A private *operating foundation* is a charity that directly conducts charitable programs through its own personnel and facilities. Such a foundation must expend at least three percent of the average value of its asset base of the prior year on its programs. If either type of private foundation holds a large block of stock that pays dividends insufficient to fund required distributions or expenditures, that foundation will be forced to dispose stock each year.

   If the stock the private foundation must sell is in a bear market, the value of the stock during the prior year will be higher than the current year in which the foundation must make the distribution or expenditure. This will increase the number of shares of stock the Foundation must sell, and the added selling pressure could perpetuate its bear market.

Observation

Be wary of investing in the stock of a Company that is extensively held by a cash poor private foundation. This observation applies to such companies as Johnson & Johnson and Microsoft whose founders have generously endowed private foundations bearing their name. Shareholders may well put increased pressure on Microsoft to pay larger dividends or redeem stock from the Gates Foundation. These actions would reduce the number of Microsoft shares owned by the Foundation that must leave its weak hands each year to meet the three percent expenditure requirement.

5. *Mutual funds.* Mutual funds that fall out of favor with the public must sell stock to cover actual and anticipated redemptions. The redemption price is fixed at the closing value of the fund's shares for the day of redemption. This rule makes it imperative that mutual funds anticipate redemptions rather than merely react to them. If the stocks held by a fund gap down on the opening of the day following redemptions in excess of fund share sales, the number of shares of stock that

must be sold to cover yesterday's redemptions will exceed the number of shares of stock behind each of yesterday's redeemed shares. After several consecutive days in which stock price declines are coupled with fund redemptions in excess of sales, the remaining owners of the mutual fund will find themselves playing a game of financial musical shares. Unlike the game of musical chairs, however, the last mutual fund shareholders left in the game of musical shares will be losers, not winners, because their shares will be worth nothing.

Observation

CNN/Money reported on September 12, 2003 that the fund-rating firm, Morningstar, issued a report recommending that investors consider selling their shares in mutual funds run by Janus, Strong, Bank of America and Banc One. This recommendation resulted from allegations by the New York Attorney General that these four firms had engaged in inappropriate or illegal trading. They had granted a prominent hedge fund special insider trading access to the funds at the expense of individual investors. The hedge fund did not admit or deny wrongdoing but agreed to pay thirty million dollars in restitution and a ten million dollar penalty. Is this the tip of an iceberg just off the bow of the titanic Mutual Fund industry? It should be noted, however that other mutual fund companies such as Fidelity and Vanguard recognized the potential problem in advance and put controls in place to prevent insider trading in their funds.

6. ***Non-publicly traded stock option holders.*** Weak hands holders include the owners of incentive and non-qualified stock options, especially former employees and their heirs. This group is prone to exercise the options granted to them and immediately sell the stock received from the Company treasury upon the exercise of the option.

Observation

Generally Accepted Accounting Principles (GAAP) has long permitted taxable income to be reduced by the exercise of non-qualified employee stock options. At the same time, no reduction is required in accounting income. These contrary rules increase earnings per share by reducing tax expense. This result has prompted the issuance of employee stock options by publicly traded companies covering billions of shares of stock.

The bear market put many of these options under water, i.e., the market price of the stock dropped below the option exercise price. The deleterious effect of worthless stock options on management and worker morale has caused many companies such as Lucent to change the terms of the underwater options to permit their exercise at a reduced stock price or to postpone their expiration date. This Board of Directors largess has maintained a significant weak hands supply of stock overhanging the market for these companies.

7. ***Imminent retirees.*** A very large and growing group of weak hands shareholders are the millions of workers facing retirement in the next five years (or earlier if they are laid off). This group must limit its risk of the loss of capital needed to produce retirement income. To achieve this goal stock held in portfolios, IRAs or 401K plans must be sold. The insurance industry promotes this sale by offering to convert stock sale proceeds into retirement annuities. For the annuitant who outlives the life expectancy tables used by the insurance company a lifetime annuity will be an outstanding investment.

8. ***Individual investors in a bear market.*** Having a comfort level with investments and avoiding stress are the typical individual investor's personal psychological goals. If ownership of stocks becomes too disconcerting, the investor's response is withdrawal of attention and a strong reluctance to commit any additional funds to market operations. At some point in a bear market, the discomfort with losses

becomes un*bear*able. A committed investor can be transformed into a departed weak hands shareholder who sells stock, and sells stock, and sells stock, swearing, "Never again" to become involved in the market of stocks (OC).

9. ***Individual investors in a bull market.*** When an individual investor has held a stock for the one year long term capital gains holding period there will be a strong temptation to sell and lock up the gain. All stocks that are priced well above the level of one year ago are vulnerable to this temptation acted on by investors (and their advisors) who were burned badly in the 2000-2002 bear market.

10. ***Foreign owners.*** Foreign owners of US stocks are weak hands shareholders if they hold a US stock that declines in price at the same time the dollar is declining in value against their currency.

Observation

It is possible that the bull market that began in 2003 will be ended by decisions made in Paris and Tokyo by foreign investors bailing out of US stocks. Foreigners who find US foreign policy distasteful or unacceptable could trigger this liquidation in an effort to discipline our perceived jingoistic international behavior (OC).

11. ***AE Insider sales.*** The Securities and Exchange Commission requires insiders, i.e., the management, directors, and their family members to report purchases and sales of stock in their

Company within two days of the transaction. The number of shares involved may be found on the SEC website at *sec.gov* under the Form 4 filings for each publicly traded company. This information is also available on other websites such as AOL personal finance or *finance. yahoo.* Pages for each Company on these websites have a pull down menu selection that shows insider trading. This information is worth paying attention to; AE insiders' sales are presumptively based on knowledge of the financial prospects for the Company and their conclusion that the stock is overvalued at its current price. The sale of stock by insiders may reflect not yet disclosed unfavorable news.

Conclusion

Members of the above eleven groups of weak hands shareholders own stock in nearly all companies with a recognized name. Selling by several of these groups at the same time could slow or even stop the bull market that began in 2003. In the bear market to follow, more and more stocks will struggle on large volume to gain ground only to fall of their own weight on much lower volume, and subsequently fail to return to the former rally level in a classic bear market pattern. AEs will see these "over the hill" stocks as short sale candidates after every modest run up in price. And when the AE short sellers rise to the occasion the investor will be faced not only with the presence of weak hands shareholders but also short sellers who act in concert to drive the price of a stock down.

E. Red flags

Red flags flying in 1999 and 2000 warned observant investors to take profits and head for the sidelines. Not only were price earnings ratios non-existent on secondary stocks, but the PE's that did exist were egregiously incongruent to historical norms for quality shares. Furthermore, the noise was being ignored. What noise? The following rule has stood the test of time, "When the dogs start to howl, it is time to take your money home." And the stocks of more dog companies were howling more loudly in the end stage of the 1990's bull market than at any other time in the history of the market of stocks (OC).

Observation

Fool me once, shame on you. Fool me twice, shame on me. Don't be caught with your earplugs in when the dogs start to howl in the bull market of 2003.

F. Base building

The subject of base building was introduced previously in Chapter VI. The importance of this subject to investors who wish to buy a target stock at the right time cannot be overemphasized. Stocks that have dropped from a higher price level and subsequently experience a relatively narrow trading range for an extended period are always candidates for further research. After a decline and during a period of low price volatility, owners of a stock who become discouraged with a lack of progress in its price tend to bail out. The stock thus moves to "stronger hands," i.e., owners who have determined not to sell unless either (a) the fundamentals of the Company change materially for the worse or (b) a significant price advance occurs.

The longer the continuation of the period of narrow price moves that establish the margins of the base, the greater will be the migration of stock into stronger hands. In this situation, when a new group of buyers for the stock appears in response to positive news on the Company an upward breakout in the price of its stock is almost assured (UC). The stronger hands owners are generally not sellers unless they have a significant profit. The oscillation that marks the end of the base building period in a low price stock may result in an upward price swing of 50% or more in just a few days.

Observation

AEs understand that the downside risk is limited in a base-building phase. They use the volatility generated by periodic spasms of investor interest to ride the sharp but temporary up moves in a long position and then they short the inevitable sharp downturns. Successfully implemented, this strategy results in very satisfactory percentage gains on the AEs capital (UC). And when investor demand finally overwhelms the AE short sellers in a short squeeze a beautiful breakout occurs on the chart. Profits are lush for the investor who has been a patient holder until the end of the base building period.

G. Efficient market hypothesis

Academia has a theory applicable to the market of stocks called the, "efficient market hypothesis." The students of this hypothesis have observed that weak hands shareholders and the sponsorship discussed in the next chapter exert opposing influences on stock prices. These students have also noted the effect of contra-cyclical trades by specialist AEs. They see the liquidity AEs provide as moderating the price volatility in stocks.

In theory these facts create the result of the efficient market hypothesis: the market of stocks generates a random series of price moves that are held in check by counter-balancing forces. Certainly there are exceptions, but the apologists for the efficient market hypothesis argue that the exceptions prove the rule. Stocks that "go off the chart" are influenced by impediments to the natural tendency of the market to rein in outsized price moves. Impediments to this natural tendency must underlie stocks that display high beta, i.e. a tendency to have larger moves in their price on any given day than the move in the market as a whole. If this were not so, the argument goes, the majority of stocks would move violently up and down at the same time. For the believers in the efficient market hypothesis, the overall stability of the trends in the market as a whole in the majority of stocks for the majority of the time is proof of their theory.

The efficient market hypothesis notwithstanding to the contrary, it is clear to any person who has taken off the gloves and traded stocks that most, if not all stocks, do in fact move violently both up and down from time to time during their price cycle. If anything, the natural tendency of the market, fueled by the liquidity of the AEs, is to exacerbate the volatility of the price of any particular stock when conditions are ripe for a move.

The money in play in the market of stocks is like fuel in a motorboat fed to the motor by a gravity flow system. In heavy seas, the fuel will slosh back and forth in all directions in the tank, the lines and the carburetor.

The result is that at times the motor will race and other times log down (OC).

The efficient market hypothesis is based on the assumption that the motorboat, i.e., the stock, whatever the weather conditions or its state of repair, can master the sea and thereby keep the fuel that drives her (money) in a relatively placid and steady state. This assumption is inconsistent with real world experience on the ocean and in the market of stocks.

H. Tax influenced transactions

In the social and economic scheme of things death and taxes are inevitable. But there is a significant difference in incidence and timing. Death is a single uncertain event, but December 31st and April 15th repeat every year.

1. *Tax selling.* The taxable year for individuals ends December 31st. Many investors clearly recognize the time value of the tax dollars they will pay to the IRS on the following April 15th. To minimize taxes due, stocks *held at a loss* may be sold in December to offset gains already realized. After waiting thirty days to avoid the "wash sale" prohibition in the Internal Revenue Code, the stock sold prior to December 31st can be repurchased. This may account for the observed phenomena that high beta stocks tend to increase in price in January relatively more than in other months as

December wash sale sellers replace the stock in their portfolios.

The opposite tax selling result arises with respect to stocks *held with a gain.* A shareholder will generally sell appreciated stock in January rather than in December in order to defer the gain into the new tax year thereby postponing the required income tax payments for twelve months to the following April 15th.

2. *Dividends vs. capital gains in the 1990's* The Federal income tax landscape encouraged the bull market of the 1990's. During that era, long-term capital gains (LTCG) rather than dividend income was tax favored. The tax on both dividends and LTCG in 1990 was 28%. But thereafter the rates began to diverge. In 1991 the maximum tax on dividends increased to 31% and in 1993 the maximum tax on dividends was further increased to 39.6%. In 1997 Congress reduced the tax on LTCG to 20%. This spread in tax rates between the maximum rate of 39.6% and 20% or *19.6%* was a powerful incentive for investors to purchase stocks for LTCG and a distinct disincentive to purchase stocks to obtain dividends. It also encouraged companies to not pay dividends but instead, to repurchase shares on the market.

3. **Current tax landscape.** The third Bush tax cut, enacted effective in 2003 has dramatically altered

the tax landscape for investments. The tax disadvantage of dividends vs. LTCG has been wiped out. Both forms of income are now taxed at 15%. When the reality of the reduced tax cost on dividends hits home on April 15th, many investors may diminish their quest for capital gains and seek a more certain return from dividends. Dividend paying stocks will be in vogue in 2004 and beyond if the gains investors realized in no name, no earnings stocks without dividends in the bull market that began in 2003 are shifted into stocks like Duke Energy, Verizon and Bristol Meyers Squibb.

I. Invest funds incrementally

After making a decision to acquire a target stock, do not commit all of your funds allocated to purchase that stock at one point in time. Fortunes have been made on a dollar cost average buy and hold plan. Purchasing stock at different times guards against the possibility that you have purchased too early; if the price of the stock drops you will be able to acquire more shares with the same number of dollars. If your decision to purchase a particular stock was initially sound, and relevant facts pertaining to the Company remain unchanged, purchasing additional shares at a lower price will be beneficial to your financial health (UC). A decision to invest incrementally over time also will *force* you to purchase an appreciating stock at higher and higher prices. If not forced you will no doubt resist buying a stock that is going up in price until a lower price returns. And when the price does not come down, you will have missed the opportunity for capital growth from an appreciating stock.

Summary Observation

Of all the elements in trading or investing in the in market of stocks, timing is the only element that is totally within your control. You and you alone can decide when to buy and when to sell, and that gives you the ultimate power in this game.

IX. Sponsorship

A significant move in the price of any stock above its equilibrium price depends upon *sponsorship* that overcomes the effect of selling by weak hands shareholders and AE short sellers. Because of sponsorship the price of a clearly "overpriced" stock, as determined by fundamental analysis, or an "overbought" stock, as determined by technical analysis, will continue to increase. Likewise, a stock that is priced propitiously according to either its fundamentals or chart pattern will fall due to the withdrawal of sponsorship.

A. Structural sponsorship

Some companies, like W.R. Wrigley, or Berkshire Hathaway, for example, historically have had intensely loyal shareholders who are not easily stampeded into selling. This is structural sponsorship created by the culture of the shareholder group. The beta of such companies is low, i.e. the price moves compared to the market as a whole is less than a ratio of 1:1. But if a low beta company cuts its dividend the natives can become very restive. Heretofore loyal shareholders start to abandon ship and the stock may be cut adrift (OC). After an abrupt downward adjustment, the stock will establish a new lower equilibrium price, and a mighty public relations effort is required if the former shareholders are to be lured back on board.

B. Creation of sponsorship

A financial news network is ready and waiting to give free (or paid for) advertising to a star "concept" stock or group of stocks in order to create sponsorship among individual investors. To a lesser degree this news network can also cast a pall on the stock of a particular Company, a group of stocks or even the whole market of stocks. The pall news generally causes individual investors to dump shares at exactly the wrong time into the waiting hands of the AE short sellers who tend to buy back loaned stock when the public is selling (OC).

1. *The financial news network.* The financial news network has many elements including the financial press, brokers, investment newsletters, financial commentators who write for newspapers, talking heads on television, etc., etc. This network uses many devices to disseminate information including word of mouth.

2. *Roses among the thorns.* Even in a bear market hope springs eternal. The few points of light attract the attention of the financial news network. The best face is put on even meager good news and frequently the result is that enough buyers reenter the market to cause a serious rally

in the price of the selected stock or group of stocks.

C. Evidence of sponsorship

How does an investor alight and ride the sponsorship wagon before it breaks down and the AEs among the sponsors start distributing stock instead of accumulating it? In other words, how does an investor find stocks in which sponsors are building a position and avoid stocks in which the former sponsors are distributing their positions to the public? The following evidence of sponsorship at work will be helpful.

1. *The forty-dollar rule.* Stocks that move through and hold above the $40.00 price point typically will attract sponsorship. AE investors tend to avoid stocks with a lack of liquidity. Stocks with a price above $40.00, generally speaking, are more liquid, i.e., more easily sold at "the market" in a large block than stocks selling below $40.00. Institutional AEs perceive stocks selling above $40.00 per share to carry lower risk; a decline in price represents a smaller percentage loss than a decline of the same dollar amount per share in a low-priced stock. For these reasons, higher-priced stocks attract AE investor sponsorship more easily than lower-priced stocks (UC).

2. *Manipulation.* If there are widespread public pronouncements from AE financial analysts

working for banks, brokers, and other financial institutions about the promise of a stock, the stock's former sponsors are probably in a distribution mode. Sponsors accumulate stock before the good news machine gets cranking and distribute that stock to the public when the favorable publicity from the tout industry is flowing briskly. The public becomes the target of both a public relations blitz and psychic pressure to buy at the same time the former sponsors decide to lighten up their positions (OC).

3. *Chart patterns.* A stock that experiences a quick upward re-pricing without any news that would justify the move is probably being sponsored.

4. *Sale of restricted stock.* A brief no-nonsense announcement that a Company has sold a block of restricted stock in a non-public sale at a discount reveals sponsorship.

5. *January trends.* Stocks that have the largest percentage gains during the month of January when market averages are flat or down suggest the presence of sponsorship. Investment strategies for the year are frequently initially implemented in January. Stocks losing in January when the market averages are up are losing sponsorship.

6. *Price and volume patterns.* A stock with growing volume and continually smaller upside price moves followed by price declines on

reduced volume may be experiencing a withdrawal of sponsorship. This pattern is also indicative of AE short selling into rallies.

7. ***Sponsorship and the specialist.*** AE sponsorship will decline in the face of increased short selling by the specialist who is required to maintain an "orderly" market in assigned stocks. As mentioned previously, the specialist has unlimited capacity to borrow stock held in street name, sell it and invest the proceeds in Treasury bills. AE sponsors follow the rule, "Join rather than fight the specialist."

Observation

The public is under a gray-out with respect to timely knowledge of short selling. This gives the specialist and AE confidants a decided advantage in the marketplace. If the SEC required all short sales not only to be identified when initiated, but also totaled and *the volume of short selling made public knowledge each day* (a simple matter with current technology) the odds against the small investor and small trader would be greatly decreased.

D. Types of sponsors

It is easier to see signs of sponsorship at work in the market of stocks than it is to identify the sponsors who are engaged in these market operations. However, you should look for the presence of the following types of sponsors. If these sponsors are accumulating stock or supporting the price of a Company's shares, your chances of success by investing in that stock are greatly improved.

1. ***Insider purchases.*** The Securities and Exchange Commission requires insiders, i.e., the management, directors and their family members to report purchases and sales of stock in their Company within two business days of the transaction. The number of shares involved may be found on the SEC website at sec.gov under the Form filings for each publicly traded company. This information is also available on other websites such as AOL personal finance or *finance.yahoo*. Pages for each Company on these websites have a pull down menu selection that shows insider trading. This information is worth your attention. Insiders' transactions are presumptively based on the AEs knowledge of the financial prospects for the Company. The purchase of stock by insiders may reflect undisclosed favorable news.

2. ***Founders.*** The founder of a public Company or family members who own shares of the Company have both a monetary and status motivation to buy its stock. However, the existence of a Federal estate tax tends to thwart that motivation. If the Federal estate tax termination in 2010 is made permanent,

the necessity of liquidating shares in the family enterprise to raise funds for estate taxes will disappear. Family members can then indulge their desire to accumulate family Company stock at higher and higher prices for its shares.

Observation

WalMart should benefit greatly from a permanent state tax repeal. If the billionaire family members are off the hook for estate taxes, they can cancel plans to sell WalMart stock piecemeal over the years to obtain the cash needed for estate taxes.

3. *Government.* In the Chrysler Corp. bailout of the 1980's the US government was a financial guarantor of this private company because it was considered, "Too big to fail." In 1998, moral suasion rather than direct financial assistance was applied to prevent the demise of Long Term Capital Management, (LTCM) a prominent hedge fund. US official's arm-twisted private financial institutions into hundreds of millions of dollars available to LTCM. This prevented it from going bankrupt because of massive losses caused by inept and reckless speculation in the currency markets. Both the Secretary of the Treasury and the Federal Reserve Chairman determined that the bankruptcy of LTCM would

have unacceptable ancillary effects on US finan-cial markets. Subsequent to the LTCM caper, there have been published reports of govern-ment support for the market of stocks through the clandestine purchase of call options on stock indexes. As explained in Chapter IX, the sellers of publicly traded options hedge their positions by the immediate purchase of the underlying security.

4. *The issuer.* The Boards of Directors of some com-panies authorize the repurchase of stock on the open market. This is helpful deep pocket's sponsor-ship when it reduces a Company's outstanding stock by more than the number of shares sold by employees exercising their stock options.

5. *Dividend reinvestments.* An indirect source of Company sponsorship comes from dividend reinvestment plans (DRIPs). Generally, these plans purchase stock for a shareholder on the open market without commission. Not to be out-done, brokerage firms now routinely offer divi-dend reinvestment in Company stock to their customers at little or no commission.

Observation

The reduction in the regular tax on dividends to 15% was established by an amendment to the Internal Revenue Code of 1986 by the 2003 Tax

Act. The reduction in the alternative minimum tax on dividends to 15% was authorized by a *single sentence in the Conference Committee Report explaining the 2003 Tax Act*. This tax cut is almost certain to encourage increased participation in DRIPs. Lower income taxes on dividends will require a shareholder to come up with less cash to pay tax on the dividends locked up in a DRIP.

6. ***Individual investors.*** The money invested in the market of stocks by individual investors tends to gravitate to stocks familiar to the investor. A decision to purchase additional shares of a Company already in your portfolio will be much less stressful than adding shares in a new Company.

Observation

Purchasing additional shares in a Company throughout a bear market will reduce your average cost basis per share in that stock. Purchases of stock for this reason, to reduce average cost basis in the portfolio, may account for the dramatic price increases during 2003 in hundreds of Nasdaq issues without earnings or general name recognition. Whether the price increase in these stocks will continue remains to be seen. Time will surely tell whether these increases were merely a dead cat bounce.

7. ***Index equity mutual funds.*** When a Company is included in a particular stock index for the first time, the index mutual funds investing in stocks included in that index will have to acquire a proportionate amount of its stock. This required sponsorship generally boosts the share price. Likewise, a Company whose stock is dropped from an index automatically loses sponsorship and the downward trend in the price of that stock is thereby exacerbated. If the stock price of the Company's replacement in the index increases, the shareholders of the index fund will benefit. The deletion of the poorly performing stock from the fund will have served its purpose.

Observation

In 1928 the number of companies included in the Dow Jones Industrial Average was increased from twenty to thirty. Since then, forty additional companies have shared the glory of being a DJIA component. The periodic purging of this index gives incentive to investors to purchase shares of a DJIA index mutual fund. They can see that loser companies, like repulsive financial tar babies, will not be allowed to fasten failure on the fund's portfolio. But does a periodic housecleaning of the dogs dragging down the DJIA call into question the validity of the current level and the trend of the index? Doesn't shuffling the deck, which is SOP when a Company in the index gets into financial trouble, falls into desuetude, or disappears entirely, create a disingenuous discontinuity in the data represented by the DJIA (OC)? And what does this discontinuity mean for the reliability of chart formations in the DJIA as a predictor of the future direction of that average?

8. *Managed equity mutual funds.* Individual investors, pension funds and charities are the principal shareholders of equity mutual funds that hold investment decision-making power over an estimated 2 trillion dollars. Incredible as it may seem, there are more equity mutual funds with shares for sale than separate companies listed on the New York Stock Exchange. But the results for managed equity mutual funds, i.e., funds whose managers select stocks for purchase and sale, are dismal. Seventy five percent of all managed mutual funds *under-perform* the S & P 500 Index over any five-year period.

Observation

The expertise of mutual fund portfolio managers is a weak reed upon which to lean to guide your investment decisions. But if, out of curiosity, you want to learn which mutual funds are winners and which are losers in any particular year, the ratings and information issued by Morningstar or Lipper Analytical Services will be useful. A study of this material shows that past performance for a mutual fund is no guarantee of future results. This argues against a buy and hold strategy for managed mutual funds.

9. *Sponsorship by institutions.* Financial websites usually have a screen showing the amount of institutional and insider ownership for any listed stock. Growth in ownership by institutions such as investment bankers and hedge funds is indicative of increasing AE sponsorship. But if institutions already own the vast majority of the shares of a particular Company, what does this portend for the price?

Observation

Perhaps institutional owners might engage in buying and selling to each other to support an equilibrium price or cause a break out. But the securities laws frown on collusion, and a bear market can chew up even stocks predominantly owned by institutions. A case in point is Pathmark, Inc. While the stock of this company is 80% owned by institutions, its price took a swan dive from $25.50 to $2.61 in 2002, followed by a rise in 2003 to $9.33, and then a plunge to $4.43.

10. ***Dollar cost averaging buyers.*** If the downtrend in a name stock has been long and severe, the ensuing up-trend may be buoyed by the sponsorship of patient and persevering shareholders who continue to periodically invest a fixed amount of money in a dollar cost averaging investment strategy.

11. ***Hedge funds.*** More than 500 private partnership hedge funds are now conducting stock market operations with an excess of 600 billion dollars. This group of buyers can provide considerable sponsorship. However, hedge fund holdings in a particular sector are usually matched by a short position in companies in that same sector. The companies whose stock is sold short are considered by the hedge fund managers to be the weakest in the sector. This is the "hedge" many hedge funds enter into. As a mandatory short seller, hedge funds constitute a group of weak hands shareholders as well as being sponsors.

12. ***AE traders.*** AE traders continually jump on and off the bandwagon for any stock. These traders are satisfied with repeated small short-term capital gains taxed as ordinary income. AEs jumping off the bandwagon and flipping their positions from long to short will result in an increase in the stock's beta. This is a characteristic not conducive to a consistent up-trend in price.

13. *AE investors.* AE investors tend to accumulate stock in a Company when the public is not buying. This untimely sponsorship generally reverses at some point after the public has returned to the market of stocks to seek its fortune.

14. *AE insider purchases.* AE insiders' purchases are presumptively based on knowledge of the financial prospects for the Company and their conclusion that the stock is undervalued at its current price. The purchase of stock by insiders may reflect not yet disclosed favorable news.

Summary Observation

If you can identify growing sponsorship for a stock and ride the sponsor's coattails, as long as they last your wealth will grow effortlessly.

X. Publicly Traded Stock Options

While this chapter deals with transactions in options on stocks, the ingenuity of the financial community has created options, otherwise known as financial derivatives, on all manner of financial products that can have a buyer and a seller. These include options on: US Treasury bond futures, dollar index futures, stock indexes, commodity futures contracts, foreign currencies, etc. etc.

Observation

All financial derivatives, including stock options, serve an economic purpose. They enable the owner or purchaser of the underlying stock, bond, commodity or currency to protect against an adverse price change in that investment. Financial derivatives were not invented simply to give traders an attractive opportunity to earn leveraged gains. And in what is essentially a zero sum game with fat commissions for the house, the gains of the few are exceeded by the losses incurred by many.

A. Publicly traded stock options—basic concepts and terms

A publicly traded "call" option is a contract to buy one hundred shares of a particular stock (the underlying stock) at a specified price per share (the exercise price). A publicly traded "put" option is a contract to sell one hundred shares of a particular stock (the underlying stock) at a specified price per share (the exercise price). The option contract trades as a separate security on a regulated exchange such as the Chicago Board Options Exchange. The contract is time sensitive, i.e., it will expire on a stated future date (the expiration date). Selling rather than buying an option contract is called "writing" that contract.

1. *Call option contract—effects.* If you purchase a call option contract, you will have the right to demand delivery to you of the underlying stock for the payment of the exercise price at any time prior to the expiration date. If you sell a call option contract, you will be exposed to the possibility that the purchaser of the call may demand delivery from you of the underlying stock in exchange for payment of the exercise price at any time prior to the expiration date. If you own the underlying stock at the time you write the call contract, that contract is "covered." If you do not own the stock, the contract is written "naked."

Observation

A call option contract has no value on its expiration date if the price of the stock is less than the exercise price stated in the contract. If you purchase a call you must expect that the price of the stock on the expiration date will be higher than the exercise price stated in the contract. If you sell a call you must expect that the price of the stock on the expiration date will be lower than the exercise price.

2. *Put option contract—effects.* If you purchase a put option contract, the right to "put" the stock to the seller i.e., you have the right to demand that the seller pay you the exercise price in exchange for delivery of the underlying stock at any time prior to the expiration date. If you own the underlying stock at the time you write the put the contract is "covered." If you do not own the stock, the contract is written "naked." If you sell a put option contract, you will be exposed to the possibility that the purchaser of the put may demand that you pay the exercise price and take delivery of the underlying stock at any time prior to the expiration date.

Observation

A put option contract has no value on its expiration date if the price of the stock is greater than the exercise price stated in the contract. If you purchase a put you must expect that the price of the stock on the expiration date will be lower than the exercise price stated in the contract. If you sell a put you must expect that the price of the stock on the expiration date will be higher than the exercise price.

3. *Market value of option contract.* The market value of an option contract at any point in time prior to the expiration date has two components: the premium value of the time remaining until the expiration date (the time premium) and the difference between the exercise price and the current market price of the underlying stock.

4. *Option symbols.* As with stocks, each call and put option has its own individual trading symbol. This symbol is a combination of the symbol for the stock and additional letters. You must use the proper symbol for the option you wish to trade. The symbol is made up of three components: an "option root" that identifies the stock, a letter to designate the month of expiration, and a letter to indicate the price of the option. The letters for calls expiring in January through December are A through L. The letters for puts expiring in January through

December are M through X. Stock prices begin with A as 5.00, 105.00, etc. and each letter forward in the alphabet increases the price by 5.00. Thus S is 95.00, 195.00, etc. Letters U through Z are included in the option symbol to denote an option price in increments of 2.50.

5. *Expiration dates.* Publicly traded option contracts expire on the third Saturday of the month and trading in the expiring options ceases on the third Friday of the month. You can purchase regular options expiring as much as six months in the future. You can also purchase "Leaps" options on stock indexes as well as some stocks that expire more than a year from the time of purchase.

Observation

The month letter in the option root for Index options may change for some months due to a conflict with the three-letter stock name for some stocks. Your broker's web site will have an "option chains" page that shows the correct symbol, the bid and asked price, and open interest information on all traded options for each future month. You should always refer to this page before placing an order for any option.

B. Trading stock options successfully

The following rules will help you to compete successfully in the stock option arena.

1. *Entering the game.* AEs are the principal players in the publicly traded stock options market. Thus, the non-AE trader is up against formidable competition in every option transaction. You should trade options only if you have already experienced success in trading stocks. And if you are lucky enough to make a nice leveraged gain in an option transaction you must elevate your level of caution in entering into the next transaction.

2. *Purchasing a call.* Before purchasing a call, you must ask the question, "Is the window open?" This will focus your attention on whether or not an investment decision is too late.

   (a) *The window.* As previously discussed, stocks tend to make upward moves over a relatively short period of time. These moves are followed by a reduction in the amplitude of price oscillations until a new equilibrium price is established. This price or relatively narrow price range will last for a longer period of time than the larger oscillations that preceded it. For the call buyer, the window is open during the period immediately *before or only at the outset* of an upward move in the price of the underlying stock. After the move is underway, the call premium in the option contract "looks back" and expands like an accordion. In this situation the window closes for the call buyer, but the glass is clear, and the view of potential future advances in price for the stock is inviting. Mistaking the glass for an open window and jumping to buy the option will lacerate your capital.

(b)   ***Spotting the open window period.*** The successful call buyer must think counter-intuitively and recognize that a *drop* in the price of an upward trending stock is a signal to buy a call.

Observation

Generally, for a call buyer the most successful strategy is to purchase a call when a stock breaks out of its base building phase. The second most successful strategy is to purchase a call only after a decline in the price of an upward trending stock. The conservative play is to purchase a call with an exercise price that is less than the current market price of the underlying stock, i.e., an in-the-money call. This call already has an intrinsic value equal to the difference between the exercise price and the market price. The chances of losing 100% of the price paid for the call are reduced by the presence of an intrinsic value.

(c)   ***Objective of call buyer.*** The objective of the call buyer is to catch a rising stock that continues to move upward *above the exercise price* by a greater amount than the premium paid for the call. In this case, the call can be sold for a short-term capital gain.

(d)   ***Objective defeated.*** If the stock does not resume its up-trend after the purchase of a call, but continues to decline to below its exercise price at the expiration date, the call will expire worthless and the amount you paid for it will be lost.

3.   ***Selling a call.*** The call seller must take the opposite tack from a call buyer and wait for the expanded look-back premium after a rise in the price of a downward trending stock. Then the call seller should sell a call with a price below the current market price of the underlying stock, i.e., an "out of the money" call. When the stock resumes its downtrend, the value of this call will diminish, hopefully to zero, and on the expiration date the call will not be exercised. In this call the seller will realize the entire premium received from the sale as a short-term gain. If the call seller had sold a covered call, the decline in the value of the stock will economically offset the gain from the call.

(a)   ***Objective of call seller.*** The objective of the call seller is to either have the value of the call fall to zero at the expiration date or to buy the call back for less than the price paid before the expiration date. Attainment of either objective results in short-term capital gain.

(b)   ***Objective defeated.*** If after the sale of a call the stock does not resume its downtrend but advances to a price that exceeds the exercise price, at some point the call will have a market price that is more than the premium paid. Then buying back the call will result in a short-term capital loss. If the call is not bought back but is held until its expiration date, and the market value of the underlying stock exceeds the exercise price, the purchaser of the call will demand delivery of the stock.

(i)   ***Effect of defeat on covered call seller.*** If the underlying stock under a covered call must be delivered, the premium received by the call seller is taxed as short-term capital gain. The economic return is less than if the call seller simply had held the stock and sold it after the increase in price.

(ii)   ***Effect of defeat on naked call seller.*** If the underlying stock under a covered call must be delivered, the call seller must buy and then deliver the underlying stock to the call buyer. This results in a double commission and a capital loss.

Observation

It is clear that if you sell a call you can lose the profit you expected if the price of the underlying stock does fails to remain even or declines prior to the expiration date. And if the price of the stock advances you can lose big time.

4. *Buying a put.* The window is generally open more often for the purchase of a put than for the purchase of a call. A stock that is in a downward trend with successively lower highs on its chart is a good candidate for a put purchase. Wait for a rally in the price of the stock to purchase the put. Generally, this is a better strategy than buying a put when the stock price is in full retreat.

Observation

Many investors purchase covered puts on stock held in their portfolio to protect against a price decline below the exercise price. The contractual right to sell the stock to a put buyer at the exercise price will lock in your gain at the exercise price of the put. But the purchase of a covered put may also increase the tax cost on dividends paid on that stock. To be eligible for the 15% tax on dividends on a stock, you must hold that stock for more than 60 days during the 120-day period that straddles the ex-dividend date. Any days on which a put buyer could exercise the put to take delivery of your stock cannot be counted toward the 60 days.

5. *Selling a put.* The criteria for timing the sale of a put are basically the same as for buying a call. The difference in profit opportunity compared with risk argues heavily for the purchase of a call. Your maximum gain on the sale of a put is the premium received. The maximum gain on the purchase of a call is theoretically unlimited and depends only on how high the price of the stock goes above the exercise price. Furthermore, selling a put may cause you to become the owner of a block of stock that you do not want in your portfolio and to pay a buyer's commission in the process. Of course you can always incur a second commission after the stock has been put to you and sell the stock in the marketplace.

6. *Price of the time premium.* It is axiomatic It is axiomatic that the longer the period of time during which the put or call contract may be exercised the higher will be the time premium. Simply because you pay a larger time premium to secure a longer holding period prior to the expiration date, however, the likelihood of a sizable favorable move is

not necessarily increased. For example, you may purchase a call that does not expire for six months and pay a hefty premium. But if the initial move in the price of the optioned stock is unfavorable, the subsequent favorable move may only offset that initial move leaving you with a reduced time premium in the option since there is less time until the expiration date.

Observation

A person with a sufficient risk taker's mentality to successfully trade stocks options will not look for trades that require a six-month or longer period to work out. A person who is comfortable only with positions that require six months or more to bear fruit should not trade option contracts. The options game is for those with relatively short-term investment objectives.

The astute option buyer acts when a favorable move is imminent. Such a buyer will purchase the option that expires reasonably soon rather than an option that expires many months in the future. But the option buyer should generally not buy an option that will expire in less than two weeks. This time period is too short. Your earnest hope that a mighty move in the right direction in the price of a stock will occur in the last week before expiration is not likely to find favor with the option gods, i.e., the AEs who make their living from the market of stock options.

7. ***The required stock price move*** Options prices are shown on your broker's website in the "option chains" pull down menu. If you compare the price of an option with the current price of the stock this will show how far the stock must move before you will realize a profit on your trade. A cursory comparison will demonstrate that a serious favorable move in the price of a stock is usually required to double your investment in the option contract. This means that most of the time, buying options is a very difficult game because the large favorable move required in the stock does not occur all that frequently. As we have noted, much of the time the price of a stock is oscillating around its equilibrium price. And, when the requisite large move in the price of the optioned stock does occur, it may reverse on a dime and wipe out your paper profit in the option before you can act.

8. **Use technical analysis** To be a successful options trader you must be a skillful and intuitive chart reader. Technical analysis is necessary for the call buyer to spot a stock whose price is trending upward to permit purchase of calls on a price decline. The put buyer must use charts to spot a

stock whose price is trending downward to permit the purchase of puts on a price advance.

Observation

A stock must be temporarily overbought (at a resistance level) for you to buy a put and temporarily oversold (at a support level) for you to buy a call. This requires your attention to the price of the underlying stock and the option several times each day unless you enter an order with your broker to liquidate the option at a predetermined price.

C. Effect of publicly traded options on the market of stocks

1. Hedging by the market maker. If you place an order with our broker to purchase a call or to sell a put, the order is submitted to the AE option market maker(s) in that stock. Upon filling the order to open your position, the market maker(s) will simultaneously purchase the underlying stock to eliminate the risk of a rise in the price of that stock.

If you place an order with you broker to purchase a put or to sell a call, the order is submitted to the AE option market maker(s) in that stock. Upon filling the order to open your position, the market maker(s) will simultaneously sell the underlying stock short to eliminate the risk of a decline in price of that stock.

2. *Purpose of the hedge.* The market maker works on the spread between the bid and asked price for an option and the certainty that the premium will shrink as time marches on toward the expiration date. The market maker is not interested in seeking reward or accepting risk from a change in the price of the underlying stock but endeavors to make a certain return on each transaction.

3. *Impact on stock price.* Because the market maker hedges by entering into transactions in the underlying stock, opening an options position will reinforce the desired trend in the price of the stock. However, when you close your position to realize a gain, the market maker must simultaneously close the hedging position. This creates market pressure that is contrary to your initially desired trend. Of course, since you are out of the option this effect is a matter of indifference to you. But closing the market maker's hedge may replace the open window of opportunity with clear glass on options at a different exercise price. AEs pay close attention to the inflating and deflating balloon of options outstanding on their stock as a tip off to a reversal in its price trend.

Summary Observation

To successfully trade options you must develop the ability to act in a counter-intuitive manner. This means selling a call during a temporary short-term up trend in the price of a declining stock and buying a call either as it breaks out of a base building phase or during a temporary short-term down trend in the price of an advancing stock. This means selling a put during a temporary short-term down trend in the price of an advancing stock and buying a put during a temporary short-term up trend in the price of a declining stock.

Never buy a call without asking the question, "Am I acting too late?" Never buy a put without asking the question, "Am I acting too early?" The answer to either question cannot be known with certainty, but at the least asking the question will give your decision-making process proper direction.

To conduct this stock market operation successfully you must become insulated from the AEs psychic noise and eliminate doubt from your mind after you have made a decision.

XI. The US Economy

The eight hundred pound gorilla in the room with every investor is the US economy, and, to a lesser extent, the economies of its major international trading partners. The macro-economic factors of importance to investors and traders include, but are not limited to such items as: interest rates; inflation; year-to-year changes in gross domestic product; balance of payments deficits; the relationship between the dollar, euro and yen; agricultural commodity prices and output; retail sales; housing starts; paper box board production; etc., etc. A complete list of important macro-economic factors, if indeed a complete list could be compiled, would be too extensive for coverage in this Book.

Interest rates are discussed in paragraph C below. Two additional macro-economic factors, important to your investment decisions, *cost imposition* and *dollarization,* are also discussed in this Chapter. Economists and policy-makers have given these factors minimal recognition. Hopefully, this explication will focus more attention on them.

A. Cost imposition

Ever larger amounts of the US gross national product are produced by sectors of the economy that have the power to impose their costs without market restraint on the other sectors. A number of these cost-imposition sectors are discussed below.

1. *Crime.* The economic and psychological costs imposed by the crime sector of the economy, organized and otherwise, are a massive deadweight that drains the production away from millions of workers and limits our prosperity. The Ten Commandments include: "Thou shall not steal; thou shall not kill; thou shall not covet." These Commandments are values any society must tenaciously enforce in its laws; these values underlie private property rights and personal security without which there can be no economic progress. The glamorization of crime on TV ("The Sopranos"), in movies ("Batman"), and on stage ("Chicago") must not be allowed to distort the truth. Crime has a totally pernicious effect on the wealth creation and distribution process in our country.

Observation

Both Federal and state governments have spun wildly OC in their emphasis on the punishment of crime rather than crime prevention.

This emphasis is costing us dearly in the expenditure of manpower and dollars. This includes:

- Extensive federal, state and local police forces dedicated to crime control.

- Byzantine procedural safeguards for criminals interpreted from the Constitution by the US Supreme Court and requiring an army of public defenders and an equally well staffed army of opposing public prosecutors at the Bar.

- Massive and ever-expanding incarceration facilities that aggrandize the life style of many of prisoners and give them an incentive for recidivism.

2. *Terrorism.* The post 9/11 War on Terrorism both at home and abroad is another heavy and nearly economically indigestible layer on the cake of costs imposed by criminal activity. For investors anticipating higher stock prices, another major terrorist attack on US soil would be a shocker. Such an "event out of left field" would certainly derail the bull market that began in 2003.

3. *Tort awards.* A very large and growing cost imposition sector in the US economy is the increasingly onerous jury awards and out of court settlements in personal injury, wrongful death, age discrimination, medical malpractice, and a multiplicity of other tort lawsuits. Consider the

1.4 million dollars recently reported in the press that was awarded to a 94 year-old woman who broke her hip from a fall in an elevator that had come to rest a few inches below floor level.

Observation

The tort awards cost imposition sector is driven by the trial attorney's guild and is funded by insurance payouts. As certainly as night follows day, insurance premiums rise inexorably. The insurance industry cries crocodile tears over the increasing volume of awards and settlements. At the same time, legions of commission compensated workers in the insurance industry receive their share of the ever-growing river of cash flowing through its accounts.

4. *Medical care.* Perhaps the largest of all cost imposition sectors is the medical care juggernaut driven by the "most effective" treatment standard. If health care practitioners do not adhere religiously to this standard, a patient can literally sue for a broken fingernail. But since the most effective treatment standard is constantly changing in the war of words waged against health care providers by lawyers, the providers are fighting a losing battle. While the providers treat one illness, the legal system invents a correlative "syndrome" caused by the treatment and spawns another round of lawsuits.

Observation

Year after year, the result of the face-off between the medical and legal professions is alarming increases in both medical malpractice insurance premiums and the charges for health care, even for the most rudimentary ailments. In a futile attempt to avoid being named defendants in lawsuits physicians test and retest their patients in the practice of defensive medicine. Financial victims of this inefficiency include venerable old-line companies like Goodyear Tire and Rubber where the costs of union and management retirees' health care benefits have gone completely OC.

5. *Public sector workers.* The cost imposition from public sector workers arises in two ways:

    (a) *Compensation.* Pay and benefits funded by tax dollars include inordinately expensive defined benefit pension plans. Such plans have gone the way of the dodo bird in all non-cost imposition sectors of the economy; and

    (b) *Regulatory burden.* The work of public sector employees creates an ever more burdensome regulatory environment for the non-cost imposition sectors.

Observation

The restrictions crafted by public sector employees are OC. The Code of Federal Regulations communicates these restrictions in over 100,000 pages and counting. These restrictions are another bonanza for the legal profession. Lawyers are richly rewarded for defending against the regulatory schemes of the third estate.

6. ***Worker's compensation claims.*** "Across the country, the cost of worker's compensation insurance is soaring at the highest rate in nearly a decade, adding yet another heavy burden on businesses and the struggling economy." *New York Times*, June 23, 2003, 1.The article attempts to explain the increase partly on the plummeting value of the insurance companies' investment portfolios. This explanation is contradicted by bull market in bonds driven by interest rate declines. Insurance companies are heavily invested in both corporate and government debt instruments.

Observation

In point of fact, the attorney-induced explosion of worker's compensation claims has been the primary motor of this major imposed cost chipper that is pulverizing the profits of US business. The only way to control this OC cost, as pointed out in the *Times* article, is to reduce payroll. This is one of the reasons for the current "jobless recovery" and the outsourcing of millions of technical jobs to countries like India that have no worker's compensation insurance, health insurance or any other form of fringe benefit for that matter.

7. ***Result of growth in cost imposition sectors.*** The circular and interrelated demand creation and reward system of the several cost imposition sectors described above is squeezing the economic value out of the non cost imposition sectors in the US economy. Enterprises in these sectors must bear the imposed costs and simultaneously compete in a market environment where their costs cannot be passed along by the, "Take it, you can't leave it," method of the cost imposers. These enterprises find it increasingly difficult to grow their profits in an economy that allows the cost imposition sectors unlimited and self-generating growth. Transferring jobs overseas is one way the non-cost imposition sectors can fight back.

Observation

When a new economic theory is developed from an examination of what went wrong with the US economy in the post-2003 bull market era, a large component of that theory will be devoted to measuring the magnitude of the cost imposition sectors and the desultory economic effect of the sand these sectors pour into the machinery of wealth creation.

B. Dollarization

The current economic growth of the US is due to the continued expansion of our money supply by the Federal Reserve and the bargain basement interest rates at which that money is being made available to consumers and business. This is being accomplished through large increases in reserves made available to the banking system at a subsidized cost (interest rates below the rate of inflation) and the Fed's direct purchase of Treasury debt.

The Fed-promoted policy of cheap and plentiful dollars and the ever-cheaper dollar resulting from the US Treasury's dollarization of the world policy should raise many concerns. For example, continued real (as opposed to inflationary) economic growth in the face of this fiscal and monetary stimulus depends upon the continued acceptance of the dollar, both in the US and by foreigners, who are the beneficiaries of the OC balance of payments deficit.

1. *Dollar sphere country acquiescence to dollarization.* Now that US currency has become more difficult to counterfeit due to its watermarks, micro printing, threads, etc., some countries such as

Argentina have thrown in the towel and the merchants and populace there accept US greenbacks as a circulating medium of exchange in preference to the peso.

2. ***Non-dollar sphere country acquiescence to dollarization.*** Many countries view the dollar as having the underpinnings enjoyed by the British pound during the period after the Franco-Prussian war in the 1870's up until WWI. At that time, the British Crown had a strong, and generally recognized as legitimate, military presence throughout the world. The sun did not set on either the British Empire or its navy. The same can be said with respect to the US military in the year 2003.

Observation

As long as the US is able to effectively use its military superiority beyond our borders, the dollar will be accepted in nearly unlimited amounts in exchange for goods and services from around the world. This is the lesson of WWII, Korea, Bosnia, and Desert Storm. On the other hand, our military failure in Vietnam led directly to an effective challenge of our economic right to the world's goods by OPEC. If high-tech US military superiority is incapable of maintaining law and order in the Middle East oil patch, due to terrorists bent on populating Hell by valuing their own lives even less than the lives of their innocent victims, or becomes unwelcome to the man on the street in that or the tribes in the hills in that part of the world, dollarization is in trouble. It will become increasingly difficult for the US to continue to unload dollars on the rest of the world.

3. *The result of dollarization.* The most notable result of dollarization is a US material standard of living that is the envy of the world. But, dollars arriving overseas form our imbalance of trade either must circulate abroad as currency, be held in the offshore money supply as euro dollars, or be retained as reserves by central banks, otherwise they will be repatriated to purchase US real estate, stocks and bonds and businesses. The US standard of living is thus being bought by the sale of our assets.

Observation

Over the years, real estate has been a prime destination for foreign dollars because recordation of real estate titles in county courthouses throughout the US prevents the ownership of real property from being challenged by arbitrary and self-serving private or government action. Property taxes, environmental restrictions and condemnation under laws of eminent domain are not viewed by foreigners as the threat to ownership presented by the direct taking of real property practiced from time to time by their governments.

4. ***Domestic acceptance of dollar flood.*** US citizens will be willing beneficiaries of the tax cut driven OC Federal deficits as long as there is nominal inflation in the price of most goods and services. So far we are in luck. A large portion of our goods is imported from low cost of production countries, and increasingly, key services such as the creation of software, come from overseas at bargain prices under our dollarization of the world policy. This price competition from foreign suppliers will keep inflation in check. But if the lynch pins of the economy, oil and natural gas, go on a price rampage that is not temporary, inflation will return and investors in these sectors will prosper.

5. ***The Niagara Falls of dollarization.*** Some time after the baby boomers reach retirement age *en masse* in 2010 and subsequent years, the Social Security Administration and the Medicare Administrations (SMA) will ask the US Treasury to return the excess trillion dollars of social security (FICA) and Medicare taxes collected by the IRS since the 1980's. The Treasury spent these dollars under the unified budget for general government operations. However, the tax cuts at the

base of the Republican fiscal policy, if made permanent, insure that the US Treasury will be a net borrower for the indefinite future of dollars to cover red ink in the Federal operating budget. There will be no surpluses to share with the SMA. To avoid massive disruptions in the US government bond market and much higher interest rates, the Federal Reserve will have to monetize the SMA's deficits through purchases of US government debt. The resulting increase in the money supply will be an unprecedented event in US fiscal history.

Observation

One benefit of the bear market and the collapse of interest rates was the chilling effect of these events on various politicians' proposals to "reform" Social Security by reducing FICA taxes and permitting workers to invest the reduction in stocks. This "reform" would have made an impossible cash flow conundrum for the SMA even worse.

6. ***Stocks that will benefit when dollarization creates inflation.*** Stocks that have balance sheet intrinsic value due to the ownership of income producing assets will benefit when dollarization creates inflation. Benjamin Graham's "value investing" will come back into favor.

   (a) ***Intrinsic value regulated companies.*** These stocks include companies in regulated industries that produce electricity and transport vital energy sources such as electricity and natural gas. Regulators will allow the pass through of increased costs plus a mark up that always accompanies a higher cost structure justified as necessary to preserve and expand a capital base essential to the operation of the economy.

(b)   *Consumables stocks.* Stocks of companies that sell branded consumables will be attractive issues in an inflationary environment. Consumers may cut back on capital purchases but their consumption of preferred consumables will continue. The household budget will always accommodate snacks, soft drinks, and an outing at McDonalds or Starbucks.

(c)   *Intrinsic value assets and their producers.* A shift in the US public's attitude toward precious metals as a store of value, even to the point of using "e gold" accounts that resurrect the use of this metal as a medium of exchange, would give a real boost to the stocks of all precious metal producers. Such a sentiment would align the US public with the thinking of the vast majority of the world's people who are too deeply embedded in poverty to purchase this precious metal. However with the prosperity of the middle class in both India and China on the rise thanks to US trade deficits with these countries, an enormous consumer demand for gold is building.

Other intrinsic value asset stocks that will benefit from the flight of capital to tangible wealth will be those of oil and natural gas producers with reserves, timber companies and other enterprises that own developed and undeveloped real estate.

7. *The lure and allure of gold.*

Lay not up for yourselves treasures upon earth where moth and rust doth corrupt.... (Holy Bible, Matthew 6:19, KJV)

(a) *Permanence of gold.* This biblical injunction ignores the fact that the metallic "barbarous relic", gold, unlike silver, retains its luster and does not oxidize under any known climatic condition. Thus, it has been considered a permanent and attractive store of value since the dawn of civilization.

(b) *Supply and demand.* The price of gold has changed over the centuries in response to supply and the demand for its use as a monetary, household and more recently, industrial metal. The flood of gold brought to Europe from the New World by Spain in the

15th and 16th centuries, for example, caused a dramatic reduction in its value from the days of the Renaissance.

Much more recently, 1934, a sharp rise occurred in the price of gold due to increased US government demand resulting from an Executive Order issued by President Franklin D. Roosevelt. Under a 1933 Order direction, provided, US citizens were forced to turn over all U.S. gold coins in their possession to the US Treasury at face value, or approximately $20.00 per ounce. In 1934, foreign sellers of gold, some of them bankrolled by US interests with prior knowledge of a second Executive Order authorized by an Act of Congress, were paid the newly established price of $35.00 per ounce for all gold they exported to the US.

(c)　*Significance of Fort Knox.* The gold hoard at Fort Knox, the largest quantity of gold ever assembled in one place in the history of the world, originated from Roosevelt's Executive Order. The Fort Knox hoard stands in the way of an OC gold price in the near future, an event that would diminish President Bush's chances for reelection.

(d)　*Predictable events.* From a technical standpoint the last twelve years have been a base building period for gold at a price between

$300 and $400 per ounce. A confirmed breakout from this base will attract the attention of high rollers everywhere who realize that many major gold mining companies have already sold a large portion of their future production. The most important causes of the coming gold price rise, however, will be a call by the central banks for the tons of gold they have "leased" to private interests and the termination of the mintage of bullion gold coins by the US mint, effectively announcing that Fort Knox has shut its doors. Upon the confluence of these events a definitive breakout in the price of gold will occur. As with Roosevelt's Executive Order, will insiders privy to the timing of these events establish their gold positions in advance and thereby profit handsomely?

Lay not up for yourselves treasures upon earth.... Where thieves break through and steal. (Holy Bible, Matthew 6:19, KJV)

Observation

In the coming bull market for gold, shares of companies with proven gold reserves will continue to offer a profit opportunity. But you must recognize that these are low or no dividend, one-product, high fixed cost, capital and labor-intensive companies that frequently experience negative operating efficiencies with higher unit sales. The *anticipation of an increase in the price of gold* is the sole reason for an increase in the price of gold mining stocks. After gold is re-priced upward, these companies will flame out. Their bull market will end when the next equilibrium price for gold of $600 per oz. is established well below the oscillation peak of $1,000 per oz for this metal.

C. Interest rates

The current historically low level of interest rates and the trend of those rates, are major determinants of stock prices.

1. ***Key interest rates.*** The most economically significant interest rates include: the prime rate at which the most credit worthy businesses borrow; the long term government bond rate, which represents an investment that is free of the risk of default; the 30 year home mortgage rate, which drives the residential real estate market; and the Federal reserve discount rate, the rate at which banks borrow funds from the Fed.

    A short term interest rate charged on more borrowed money in the economy than the Federal Reserve's discount rate is the federal funds rate. This is the overnight rate set each day by the Federal Reserve to govern loans by banks with excess reserves to banks short on reserves. Other important short-term rates are the rates paid on money market accounts and Treasury bills in which sidelined cash is waiting for investment.

2. *Correlation between rates.* To add to the complexity of the interest rate picture, you should realize that short-term and long-term rates do not always move in the same direction much less are they in lockstep. The spreads between the several important interest rates, how these spreads influence capital flows, and the recycling of US trade deficit dollars into government bonds is the subject of a separate book that will have to be rewritten periodically. The discussion on interest rates in this Chapter provides less esoteric rules that are both reliable and useful in a traders or investor's decision-making process.

3. *Rising interest rates.* In a rising interest rate environment, stock prices will drop. A practical reason for this result is that interest-paying investments become more competitive. A more theoretical reason is that higher interest rates cause a concomitant increase in the discount factor used to determine the present value of future earnings or cash flow. A higher discount rate drives the present value of the future earnings and cash flow down and thus reduces the intrinsic value of the stock.

Other reasons for lower stock prices when interest rates rise are both clear and practical. Companies with large debt will have increased interest expense and reduced profits. And as the cost of borrowing increases, consumer spending will decrease, aggregate demand in the economy will drop, and corporate profits will shrink.

Observation

A stock market adage is that on the third increase in the discount rate by the Federal Reserve the stock market will stumble. It is not the effect on short-term interest rates of this Fed action that is the only damper on stock prices. This action generally signals a tightening of money supply growth. On the other hand, when long-term bond rates increase due to market forces, investors tend to sell bonds to avoid further capital losses. If these investment funds are redirected to equities, share prices will rise.

4. *Falling interest rates.* Declining interest rates cut several ways in their effect on stock prices but the overall result will be favorable.

    (a) *Cause competition from real estate.* Lower interest rates attract large amounts of capital into one of the stock market's chief competitors for investment dollars, real estate.

Observation

President Ronald Reagan's Economic Recovery Tax Act of 1982 (ERTA) allowed the eighteen-year double declining balance depreciation method to be used for the first time by owners of commercial real estate. ERTA also continued to permit the deduction of real state losses against ordinary income earned from non real estate income such as wages, interest and dividends. When the long-term mortgage rates receded from their 1982 highs of over 14%, ERTA'S accelerated depreciation was the prime mover in the sale of real estate "tax shelters" between 1983 and 1986 in the hundreds of billions of dollars. Predictably, the stock market languished.

Unlike what happened in the 1980's, the current round of mortgage interest rate reductions is having a positive rather than a negative effect on stocks. Low interest rates are inflating the price of the US housing stock thereby restoring the wealth US homeowners lost in the bear market. These rates provide the purchasing power necessary for buyers to bid up the price of housing. The resulting inflation in value of the total housing stock has permitted many homeowners to expand their consumption of goods and services by borrowing on the increased equity in their homes. This has given the economy strong consumer sector support.

Furthermore, employed homeowners with a renewed sense of financial well being have shown enthusiasm for reentering the market of stocks with funds contributed to 401 K plans and IRAs.

    (b)   ***Bring about a weaker dollar.*** Lower interest rates tend to be accompanied by a decline in the value of the dollar in terms of foreign currencies. During the declining phase foreigners are discouraged from buying US stocks denominated in dollars. Once the perception becomes general that the decline in the value of the dollar is on its last legs, however, US equities again become attractive to foreign investors. Then their stronger money has increased purchasing power over US stocks. In the meantime foreign stocks that are traded overseas as well as on US markets benefit from a weaker dollar.

    (c)   ***Cause deflation in prices.*** Declining interest rates do not cause but are evidence of a deflationary cycle in the economy. In such a cycle, the prices of goods and services in general, as well as money, are headed south. An important question is whether the profits derived from the sale of cheaper goods and services will decline as well. This depends upon cost controls implemented by management and will vary from company-to-company and industry-to-industry. The profits of Dell Computer, for example have held up reasonably well even as prices for Dell's computer products declined dramatically. For some companies with significant debt, lower interest rates mean reduced expenses and increased earnings.

Observation

Falling interest rates reduce the price the financial sector charges for its chief product, credit. This reduction in the cost to borrow promotes increased borrowing by consumers and business. Earnings should be enhanced for lenders who can keep their non-performing loans and cost of money UC. Regarding the effect on the economy, as previously noted many homeowners are borrowing against the equity in their homes at six percent for 30-year mortgages and four percent home equity lines of credit. Credit card consumers accustomed to paying eighteen percent interest are now able to borrow double the amount nine percent and maintain the same monthly payments. Inveterate credit card junkies with satisfactory credit are able to make cash withdrawals on one card and then switch the balance due in a credit card promotion to a new lender at interest rates as low as zero percent. Expansion in home equity loans and credit card debt has fueled the high level of consumer spending responsible for near record GDP growth as the US enters the quadrennial presidential follies.

    (d)   *Hit savers in their pocketbook.* Millions of retirees who count on bank CD and money market account interest to support their life styles are experiencing pain. The dramatically reduced interest on these investments has greatly diminished their ability to be consumers, savers and generous parents and grandparents. Sooner or later the siren song of higher stock prices may appeal to some of these folks.

D. Dire predictions for the US economy

   1.   *Martin Weiss.* Martin Weiss, who publishes the *Safe Money Report*, is apoplectic in his prediction of the imminent bad loan crises facing US banks. As far as he is concerned, the US banking system is a house of cards ready and overripe for collapse.

Observation

Weiss' strident warnings of an imminent financial apocalypse overlook the massive subsidy to the banks by the Federal Reserve from a one percent interest rate and unlimited liquidity. This opportunity has permitted banks to offset sour loans by very profitably borrowing short term and lending mid and long term. If interest rates return to a sustained upward trend, however, this currently expedient policy will turn on the banks like a cornered wolf, and Weiss may be proven correct in his dire prognostications. Weiss' theory is that the ensuing profit squeeze on US banks will lead to a credit crunch that will limit business and consumer loans, reduce corporate earnings and put the kibosh on the bull market of 2003.

2. *Nick Guarino.* Another even more extreme doomsayer, Nick Guarino, who writes the *Wall Street Underground* from an undisclosed foreign location, trumpets the arrival of horrendously calamitous events resulting from the collapse of the US banking system. His advice is to convert *all* financial assets (including those held in retirement plans), which represent soon-to-be bad loans from others to you, to gold, cash, euros and T Bills. You should withdraw these assets from all non-governmental financial institutions. Finally, Guarino advises his readers to head for a hideaway in the hills with their wealth in tow in order to escape the social chaos that is certainly coming to all urban areas. But in this hasty departure, do not forget to send your forwarding address to the publisher of his newsletter.

Summary Observation

A group of economists meeting in solemn assembly might not be able to even agree on the time of the sunrise. Turning to this profession for guidance in your investment decisions will not be fruitful. It is your personal economy that must be given attention. What is the unemployment rate among you, your friends and family? How many in this group are buying a larger house or new car? Is your bank busy when you make a deposit or use the ATM card? When you go out to eat what price for a meal seems too expensive? These and other similar types of personal experiences telegraph optimism or pessimism toward economic prospects. And it is the measure of those sentiments on a broad scale that drives future economic behavior and the direction of the market of stocks.

XII. Future US Society

Too much attention on the old growth economic forest will be dangerous to the value of your investments. Do not ignore the new shoots and saplings that may grow to dominate the landscape of the US society in the years ahead.

A. Change in family values

The American Civil Liberties Union and other activists intent on making their mark on US society, along with leaders of main line churches committed to inclusion, an activist judiciary, and many members of the public are all putting increased politically correct pressure on governments and business to recognize and subsidize the partnering of: women and men outside of marriage, men and men, and women and women. Increasingly, these partnerships are being modeled as attractive "alternate" lifestyles by the US entertainment industry. Not wanting to be left behind, the US educational industry is bringing the new morality into the classroom so that our children will enter their adult lives with little appreciation for the pivotal role the nuclear reproductive family has played in our culture.

1. ***Economic effect on housing.*** The major capital investment in the United States, its housing stock designed primarily for the occupation by families with children, will have diminished economic utility if the cultural norm becomes the union of unmarried childless individuals. Millions of four and five bedroom homes built to serve the needs of an entirely different value system will be in excess supply. Declining residential real estate values and mounting foreclosures will force the Federal Reserve to deliver massive liquidity props to the mortgage industry.

2. ***Ancillary economic effects.*** The economic needs of the nuclear family throughout US history have spurred the breadwinning activities of fathers and more recently, mothers alike. If any social transaction other than war has powered the economy, it has been family formations. The already overbuilt import and retail industries, primarily established to provide the consumer goods necessary to provision expanding numbers of families, will crash and burn when the growth stops.

Observation

If the family incentive for production and the family imperative for consumption diminish, growth in aggregate demand will slow and the

US gross national product could well shrink rather than expand.

B. Planned permanence

A self-destructing, polluting, gasoline guzzling, internal combustion engine will not power the automobile of the future. The fuel of tomorrow will be hydrogen and the power plant will be a fuel cell producing abundant useable energy with water as its only byproduct. Further, cars will be sold with an optional solar-powered electrolysis water-to-hydrogen fuel production unit, and both the automobile and its power production source will be purchased on long-term (10 to 15 year) financing that correlates with their useful lives. An inevitable extension of this technology will be the solar/hydrogen production of on-site energy for homes and offices.

Observation

Widespread use of hydrogen as fuel for extended-life automobiles will result in wrenching economic dislocations. As planned permanence replaces planned obsolescence for automobiles, after the existing gasoline vehicle fleet is replaced unit production will drop; Detroit's factories will go back to one shift and oil pumping and shipping will be curtailed. If the hydrogen/solar technology extends to homes and offices, the need for natural gas and electric power production and distribution systems will be drastically reduced. Billions of dollars of capital invested in all of these industries will no longer produce an acceptable rate of return. If the purchase of the components of solar/hydrogen technology adds to the OC trade deficit, planned permanence will have a further negative effect on job creation in the US.

C. Citizen consumers-not-producers

The result of many US and state government actions has been the expansion of the number of citizens without jobs who still, nonetheless, are consumers.

Here are a few of the many examples of this citizen consumers-not-producers policy that will shape the future US society:

1. *Immigrants.* The Federal government's no-protection of national borders policy is tacit acceptance of the fact that the US requires millions of illegal Hispanic immigrants to do the work its citizens will not do. This need is also met by a very sizable number of resident aliens of Indian, Chinese, and Arabic extraction holding visas for a temporary to near permanent stay in the US. The high birth rates of all of these workers and their propensity to have children within the cultural group (who become citizens at birth) will eventually cause the former

WASP or Catholic majority to become a minority in the US.

2. ***Early retirement for the military.*** Military personnel can retire after twenty years with generous pensions.

3. ***Extension of early retirement.*** The twenty years of service requirement to accrue pension benefits is being extended to homeland security positions such as police and fire protection, marshals and sheriffs.

4. ***Vacation and sick leave.*** Federal and state workers can carry over literally years of unused vacation and sick leave to accelerate their retirement date.

5. ***Workers compensation awards.*** Legislatively sanctioned worker compensation awards provide paid retirement from work for hundreds of thousands of former and now "disabled" workers enjoyed at the beach, in the garden or on the volleyball court.

6. ***The lottery jackpot.*** The no-work ethic is being aided and abetted by dozens of state government sponsored lotteries. Billions of dollars in annuities are being paid to the lucky winners, many of whom are able to leave their jobs behind.

7. ***Legalized gambling.*** The no-work ethic is also being promoted by gambling on riverboats and Indian reservations in a majority of states.

Observation

Television and movies generally make a farce out of work and portray employers as either exploiters of the underdog or feckless saps. Does life imitate art? Like the characters in a Henry James novel, there are millions of people in the US who have salubrious lifestyles without seeming to turn a tap at gainful employment. Does history repeat itself? The Romans developed the citizen consumers-not-producers economy to a high art.

D. Nanotechnology

We have seen the future and it is infinitesimal. Recording a thousand or more CDs in a cigarette pack size block of silicon is just the beginning. Welcome to the world of nanotechnology, the science of manipulating matter at the atomic level. New materials, intelligent machines and tiny devices will flow from the ultra-miniaturization that is right around the commercial corner. Will nanotechnology create as many IPO's (Inherently Putrid Opportunities) as the dot-com craze? No, because too much capital is required to be a player.

Observation

Will nanotechnology create more jobs than it destroys? At the risk of being labeled a latter day Luddite, I will say, "No." Why? The general educational level of the US public is not high enough for the vast majority to get involved with nanotechnology as paid workers. Nanotechnology will create large incomes for the gifted few, and job replacement devices that will impact the average many. Nanotechnology will bring additional pressure for the US to go further down the dollarization and citizen consumers-not-producers policy roads.

Summary observation

There is nothing so inevitable, irrepressible and immutable as change. The investor must accept this fact and make the best of it.

XIII. Direction in the Market of Stocks

Any writer on financial topics is faced with the moment of truth when addressing the future direction of the market of stocks. It would be easy to duck this issue, but that is not the author's style.

A. Prior bear markets

Harry Schultz has described twenty-three bear markets between 1900 and 1987, with drops in the Dow Jones Industrial Average (DJIA) ranging from 13.9% in 1952 to 90% in the 1929–1932 major bear. The total time the bear prowled was twenty-eight years with the average length of each bear market being 16.2 months. But averages do not tell the whole story, "After the 1929 bear, it took 26 years to recover. If that is too extreme for you, it took 14 years after the 1937 crash." Schultz, *After a Crash Bear Market Money Making,* 26. Bear markets since 1987 included the period from October 15, 1987 to January 7, 1988, and October 13, 1989 to December 5, 1990.

B. Hibernation of the bear

The bear market that commenced on September 23, 1999 ended under the Dow theory when the DJIA advanced more than 20% from its Oct 9, 2002 low of

7286 after a subsequent higher low of 7502 on March 11, 2003. It was May 28, 2003 at a DJIA level of 8743 when the technical analysts could point to their charts and state confidently that the bull market of 2003 had begun. That being said, the $6.4T question is whether the bull market that began in 2003 is here for the long term or is it a temporary reversal of the 1999–2002 bear market that so traumatized investors?

> The bear market ends when everything in the way of possible bad news, the worst to be expected, has been discounted, and it is usually over before all the bad news is 'out'. Edwards and McGee *TAST*, 19

1. *Inventory of bad news.* The inventory of bad news is far from exhausted. Still remaining in this inventory are: a jobless recovery, OC personal bankruptcies, OC Federal deficits, OC imbalance of trade, interest rates at the very nadir of the interest rate cycle, the threat of international terrorism, and an economy dependant on ever-larger imports of oil and natural gas from countries rife with radical adherents of Islam.

Observation

How influential are these macro-negatives on the price of individual stocks? It is probably asking too much of investors and traders to connect the dots between the potential for big picture bad news and the economic performance of particular companies. And even if the dots are connected some companies will actually benefit from crises that cause money to flow.

2. ***Out of stock specific bad news.*** In predicting the immediate future of the market of stocks, it is important to recognize that the culminating cause of the bear market was the exposure of massive nefarious management and accountant misbehavior in major US corporations such as Enron, Global Crossing, Tyco, World Com, etc., coupled with the inference that these practices were endemic throughout the US business community. The forthright response of Congress in requiring top management to take personal responsibility for corporate financial statements (the "Sarbanes-Oxley Act of 2002"), and the changing of the guard at the SEC, has since resuscitated investor confidence in reported earnings. The worst of the corporate credibility crises is clearly over, and a major impediment to the propagation of a bull market has been removed.

C. Money keeps the bear asleep

Until another major international or domestic shoe drops that will abort the present trend of quarter-to-quarter increases in corporate earnings, the bull market that began in 2003 has a good chance of remaining in place. Importantly, President Bush would like to avoid his father's experience as a one-term president. A favorable stock market is an important prop for a successful presidential political campaign. Therefore, to win one for the Jr. Gipper, the fiscal policy enacted by the Republican Congress will continue to pour deficit dollars into the economy. At the same time a continuation of an expansionary Federal Reserve monetary policy will continue to make those dollars very cheap to borrow. It would be most unusual for stocks to retreat in the face of this juxtaposition of fiscal and monetary stimulus of historic proportions.

Observation

As investors put more and more of the funds loafing in money market accounts and Treasury bills to serious work in equities, the market of stocks will continue upward. But like a horse sent out to plow or to pull, if too much labor is demanded neither the horse nor the money will come home at the end of the day.

D. Predictions

There is a Wall Street adage that can be applied to the progress of a bear market, "Stocks climb a wall of worry." In the first draft of this chapter, written in early 2003, I recorded my stock market forecast for the year ahead: the market of stocks would climb the wall of worry and the DJIA would reach 10,000 in 2003.

1. ***Explosion in Nasdaq stocks.*** With the DJIA at 9600 my January prediction is on target. What I did not predict as part of the bull market that began in 2003 was a 50% increase in the Nasdaq index. This rise is remarkable in light of the fact that the largest cap stock in that index, Microsoft, actually declined during the bull market that began in 2003. But the no-name Nasdaq stocks have taken off flying. The shares of literally hundreds of companies with zero earnings and paying no dividends have doubled, tripled and more since January 1, 2003. Indeed the average increase in price for all Nasdaq stocks since their bear market lows is well over 100%.

Observation

This Nasdaq phenomenon reflected investor AE accumulation by individuals, hedge funds and mutual funds and a paucity of AE trader short selling in the vast majority of Nasdaq stocks. As certainly as night follows day, there will come a time more than twelve months after the price increases have occurred when these no account stocks are promoted to the public so that their AE owners can distribute the shares at a tidy profit. In the prior bull market, many such stocks were packaged in "tech stock fund" wrappers. Watch for new trendy marketing jargon this time around such as "Nasdaq Performance Fund."

2. ***The market of stocks in 2004 and beyond.*** For the period January through October the 2004 bull market will continue. The DJIA will amaze the naysayers and reach 12,000. But the DJIA will not reach the 14,000 level it would have attained had the bull market of the 1990's continued without interruption. The Standard and Poor's 500 will enjoy a smaller but still very respectable 10-15% increase from its YE 2003 levels. The vast majority of Nasdaq stocks will face stiffer headwinds as the lush profits of the bull market that began in 2003 are harvested. After the election when interest rates are allowed to rise, the accumulation phase of the bull market that began in 2003 will run out of buyers and a distribution phase will set in. The bear will return to the market of stocks as it has so many times in the past.

E. Tomorrow's Market of Stocks

1. ***Straw in the wind.*** The *Boston Globe*, one of the premier newspapers in the US, no longer reports New York Stock Exchange transactions. The Globe's daily stock pages are titled "Unified Stocks" and include in one alphabetical listing, composite data for stocks traded on the Nasdaq,

the NYSE and AMEX exchanges. This could be merely a reflection of the rivalry between the financial communities of Boston and New York, but perhaps the *Globe* is prescient.

2. ***NYSE dominance threatened.*** The past President of the NYSE, Richard A. Grasso, resigned in 2003 amid an outcry over a deferred compensation package that was measured by some critics to be as much as one hundred and forty million dollars. Grasso's defenders justified the compensation, however, because he was able to keep electronic trading away and thus he protected exchange members. See "Under the Gun at the Big Board" *Business Week*, 10/27/03, pg. 49 As pointed out in this article, the specialist system is under severe attack by mutual funds that want to deal directly across the table in large transactions. Electronic marketplaces now in use, such as the Archipelago Exchange and Instinet, make such dealings possible.

Observation

The NYSE specialists, who are protected by the "trade through" rule, and other limiting rules under the present system, have real time information on the support and resistance levels for the stocks in their book. This knowledge tempts them to trade for their own accounts ahead of the market. This practice is forbidden fruit and the eating thereof recently discovered by New York Attorney General, Elliot Spitzer, will lead to fines in the millions of dollars, and much adverse publicity for the specialist community. The market of stocks, always trading ahead of the news, has taken the stock of the largest of the seven NYSE specialist firms, La Branche & Co, *down* to less than one fourth of its value at the beginning of 2003.

3. ***Frustration of the threat to the NYSE.*** At present, no electronic marketplace replicates the auction system where multiple buyers or sellers can make offers at the specialist's location on the floor of an exchange, or enter offers in the specialist's book at above or below market prices for later execution. The present system is touted as producing the best price for investors. This argument is self-proving. The SEC "trade through" rule requires that orders for stock be executed on the market with the best price. The rule prohibits stocks listed on the NYSE from trading away from the exchange at more than a one-cent difference in price from the last exchange trade. In other words, the ebb and flow of the market is not allowed to wash over the electronic marketplaces. These marketplaces are now relegated to being the tail wagged by the NYSE dog.

Observation

Electronic marketplaces for stocks have replaced the auction market model throughout Europe. It is only a matter of time before the NYSE auction system is supplanted by a more open, fair, and democratic market of stocks. If the SEC would: (a) permit a 2 or 3 cent "trade through" rule, (b) allow a unified electronic marketplace and (c) require a public "book" for each stock then every investor or trader would have the information now possessed only by specialists. The public book would show all open offers to buy and sell, identify and report daily share numbers of long sales, short sales, upside, and downside volume. In such a market of stocks, the playing field would be level, technical analysis can become a analytical tool, and many of the inherent advantages now enjoyed by AEs would be stripped away.

Conclusion

The author has derived his observations on the market of stocks from both the study of investment and economic literature and hands-on experience. In these intellectual, and sometimes emotional, perambulations he has learned to be humble in the face of success and persistent in learning from losses and lost opportunities, of which there have been many. If you apply these observations to transactions in the market of stocks, you will soon recognize that there are numerous variables in play at all times and these variables will frequently interact in new ways. As the Greek philosopher Heractalites once said, "One never steps into the same river twice." This observation is far more apropos than, "There is no new thing under the sun." Even the author of this Bible verse from Ecclesiastes 1:9, said to be Solomon, would be surprised by the market of stocks where both the experienced and the inexperienced investor and trader alike must expect the unexpected.

Final Observation

Has this Book suggested that participating in the market of stocks is too daunting or too difficult a task for you to master, and that you should confine your investments to shares in index mutual funds or EFTs? I hope not, but if so, you still may be encouraged to try your hand at investing in, or even trading, individual stocks if you focus on this maxim, my final observation...*for every hitchhiker there's a ride.*

Index

0-595-30319-6